GUIDE TO PRACTICAL HOLOGRAPHY

by christopher outwater
eric van hamersveld

PENTANGLE PRESS
132 Lasky Drive / Beverly Hills, Calif 90212

Copyright © 1974 by **PENTANGLE PRESS**
132 Lasky Drive, Beverly Hills
California 90212

LIBRARY OF CONGRESS CATALOG
CARD NUMBER 74-83824

ISBN #0914748—01—7

Pentangle Press, 132 Lasky Drive, Beverly Hills,
California 90212.

Second Edition, Revised, 1975.
Photo Credit to Alex Hadju.

INTRODUCTION

Both Eric and I have reviewed the litera-
ture available to the beginning holography
student. We found that most books were
either too cursory and topical in information or too difficult for a student lacking a
well-rounded physics background. We
hope that this text helps to solve that problem by being "middle of the road".

Although one does not need to know the
basic theory included in the beginning sections of this guide, we feel that even a
simple understanding of light theory and of
lasers and coherent light is extremely help-
ful in comprehending the process and pro-
cedures of holography.

All of the theory presented here leads
eventually to the more practical problems
of holography, such as isolation tables,
coherence lengths, lenses, optical mounts,
etc. The plan of the booklet is to begin
with theory and then proceed to answer
the problems that naturally arise, with
practical, low-cost solutions. Needless to
say, you will find that we include a good
number of illustrations.

We gratefully acknowledge the assis-
tance of Ralph F. Wuerker, Ph.d. in the pre-
paration of this guide to holography.

FOREWORD

At this point in time, holography seems to be all things to all people. To the mechanical engineer, it is a new means for non-destructively testing engineering structures. To the aerodynamicist, it is a means for visualizing subtle aerodynamic flows and phenomena. To the computer engineer, it is a new means for permanently storing information at high densities. To the acoustician, it has offered new insights into acoustical imagery. To the educator, it offers new possibilities in teaching and training aids. To the artist, it offers a new art form and mode of expression. To the art connoisseur, it offers a new way of transporting and displaying priceless art treasures. To the movie mogul, it offers the future possibility of true three-dimensional movies. To advertising people, it offers a new display. To security people, it offers another way for detecting intrusion. To physiologists, it offers a mechanical model of the brain, which like the hologram is also distributed in its storage of information. To legal people, it offers non-forgeable records. To metrologists, it offers a new method of measurement. To physicists, it is one of the finest expressions of the laser. To Dennis Gabor, it was the 1971 Nobel Prize in physics for an idea published in 1948.

A technique with such universal appeal and possibilities might seem to require great investment in laboratory equipment and knowledge. Such is not the case, at least for some of the simple and more enjoyable forms of holography. As will be seen from this book, holography can be practiced with rudimentary equipment and a fair amount of common sense. Outwater and van Hammersveld adequately start the fledgling holographer on the joy and practice of the technique using small, relatively inexpensive helium-neon lasers and homemade ancillary equipment. Enough physics is given to at least let one appreciate the laser and the physical properties of light upon which the hologram is based. This is the first book not written for the graduate engineer or science student. Thus, it fulfills a real need.

Holographic imagery is the most realistic form of stored imagery yet discovered. The reader will find, that unlike photographs, pictures, or even stereo-pairs, holograms have continuous depth and parallax. In addition, intensities in hologram image vary over a range of nearly a million (compared to one hundred for a photograph). All of these features contribute to the realism of the image, which is so good that in some cases, people see color even though the image is played back with a monochromatic laser. Holograms should challenge the reader's notions of perception.

Ralph F. Wuerker, Ph.D.
Palos Verdes Estates, California
March 1974

CONTENTS

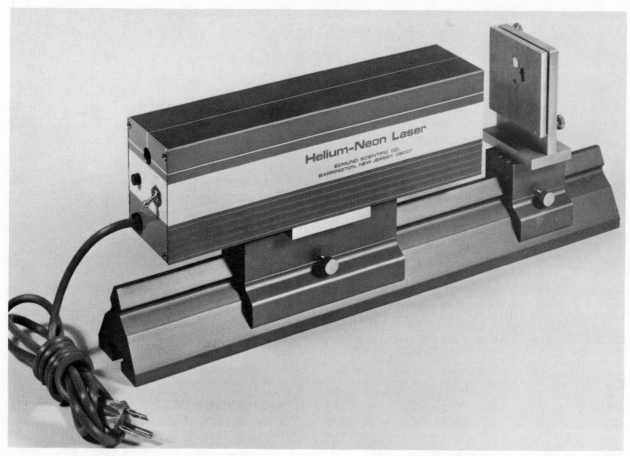

Photo Courtesy The Edmund Scientific Company

1. SOME BASIC CONCEPTS

Some of the questions about holography which come to mind immediately might serve as a good starting point for our discussion. They are: "What is a hologram? And how does holography work?" Note that the process is referred to as holography while the plate or film itself is referred to as a hologram. The terms hologram and holography were coined by Dennis Gabor (the father of holography) in 1947. The word hologram is derived from the Greek words "holos" meaning whole or complete and "gram" meaning message. Older English dictionaries define a hologram as a document (such as a last will and testament) handwritten by the person whose signature is attached.

The theory of holography was developed by Dennis Gabor, a Hungarian physicist, in the year 1947. His theory was originally intended to increase the resolving power of electron microscopes. Gabor proved his theory not with an electron beam, but with a light beam. The result was the first hologram ever made. The early holograms were legible, but plagued with many imperfections because Gabor did not have the correct light source to make crisp, clear holograms as we can today nor did he use the off axis reference beam which we will describe later. What was the light source he needed? The LASER, which was first made to operate in 1960.

Laser light differs drastically from all other light sources, man-made or natural, in one basic way which leads to several startling characteristics. Laser light can be **coherent** light. Ideally, this means that the light being emitted by the laser is of the same wavelength, and is in phase. These might be new terms for some of you, so let us form an analogy that might clarify the term **coherence.**

Let's say that you are flying over a freeway at rush hour, and directly below you is a long tunnel that all the cars must go through. Nothing is strange about the fact that all different styles and makes of motor vehicles emerge from the tunnel at differing velocities. A Cadillac at 75 mph, a Volkswagen at 45 mph, a motorcycle at 60 mph, a truck at 40. The distances between vehicles also vary. Thus you have different types of vehicles at varying speeds, and at constantly changing distances between each other.

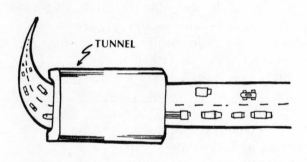

But then something very strange takes place; you see that more and more 1973 Cadillac Coupe de Villes are emerging.

No, wait, look! All the cars coming out of the tunnel are 1973 Cadillac Coupe de Villes, gold with tinted windows, exactly alike, (a situation not totally uncommon in some carefully chosen Southern California suburbs). Not only are they the same year, make and color, but they are all traveling at exactly the same speed and all bumper to bumper, never changing. So that if you just happened to have a stopwatch handy you would find that the cars are exiting at a rate of one car per second. If you were to leave, or more likely, pass out from the

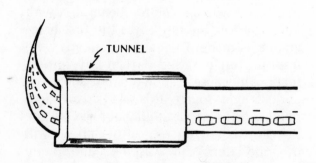

fumes, you would observe upon reawakening that the exit rate of the cars is still exactly one car per second. The cars are in phase.

The way in which coherent light is emitted from a laser is analogous. Keep in mind that although absolute 100% coherence is rarely, if ever, attained, there are certain types of lasers readily available which have sufficient coherence to make excellent off axis holograms.

The light emitted from a laser is all exactly the same type, or make, depending upon the characteristics of the substance which is lasing. I will explain in the next chapter what the term laser means, and how the laser works to give coherent light. Right now it is important to remember that the frequency of laser light is unvarying and that in the same medium, all light, i.e., light of different wavelengths or frequency, travels at the same speed.

It's true that all electromagnetic radiation, including the very small portion we call visible light, travels in a vacuum at the approximate finite speed of 186,000 miles per second. (Note, the velocity of light in a vacuum is one of nature's constants and is referred to by the letter c). Light waves can oscillate at different frequencies and with correspondingly different wavelengths so that for any given amount of time, say one second, a greater number of shorter wavelengths of (blue) light would be emitted from a laser than longer wavelengths of (red) light. This does not mean that different wavelengths travel at different speeds. Again to the freeway analogy;

given the same speed and the same distance between cars, more Volkswagens (short wavelength) than Cadillacs (long wavelengths) would pass by a point in the same amount of time.

Now is a good time to define some terms used previously but that you will see throughout this explanation. Wavelength, usually symbolized by the Greek letter λ for lambda, and frequency, symbolized by the Greek letter ν, pronounced nu, have a reciprocal relationship $\nu \lambda = C$. The shorter the wavelength, the higher the frequency and vice versa. The amplitude is the height or intensity of the wave. For example, a laser rated at 5mW (milliwatts, one thousandth of a watt) would give off light at the same frequency and wavelength as another laser of the same type rated at 1 mw. But the wave heights of the 5 mw laser light would be five times higher than that of the 1 mw laser.

The wavelength is the distance from one crest to the next; this is also one cycle. It seems logical that we would need some constant measure of time in order to count the cycles. This constant unit of time is usually one second. Thus the term cycles per second, or cps., which is often referred to as Hertz or Hz (in honor of the German physicist Heinrich Rudolph Hertz, who discovered radio waves). The oscillation frequency of electromagnetic radiation in the visible region is approximately 10^{15} Hz. Wavelengths of visible light are between 400 and 700 nanometers or billionths of a meter in length.

We have described light as energy that travels through space in a **wave** form. For our purposes in talking about holography this is the case. However, the theory of light is not all that simple. The fairly recent history of the theory of light has unfolded miraculously, involving such great minds as Isaac Newton, Thomas Young, Christian Huygens, Max Planck, Niels Bohr and, of course, Albert Einstein. Still, the dual characteristics of light remain one of the many puzzles of nature. The particle-wave problem which we refer to was clarified somewhat in the year 1900 when Max Planck proposed that all electromagnetic energy is radiated in discrete packages which he called quanta, or singular quantum. Einstein later confirmed Planck's theory via the photoelectric effect and used the word photon to refer to these energy packages. Scientists today refer to light sometimes as particles (photons or quanta) and other times as continuous waves depending on the situation or experiment. The problem is not with nature but with our models or concepts of nature. It is always very important to remember not to let your idea or model of the way anything **should be** usurp the place in your mind of the way **it is** or **might be.** That place should always be open for new information whether it agrees with theory or not.

CRESTS

TROUGHS

- RISING AND FALLING AT RIGHT ANGLES TO DIRECTION = TRANSVERSE WAVES

Light travels in a wave form. More precisely, a transverse wave form. The crests and troughs of the waves (which in the case of light are electromagnetic fields) are rising and falling in a direction at right angles to the direction of travel. A swell or wave in the ocean is a good example of transverse wave motion. You'll notice that the rising and falling action of the wave is at right angles to the direction of travel.

A simple proof of the wave theory was first demonstrated by an English physician named Thomas Young in 1802.

He forced the light from a single light source to pass through a narrow slit and then forced that same light to pass through two more narrow slits placed within a frac-

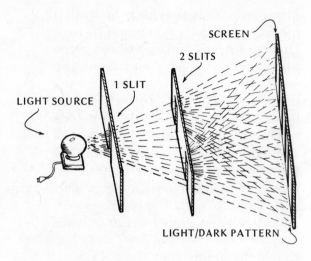

SCREEN

2 SLITS

1 SLIT

LIGHT SOURCE

LIGHT/DARK PATTERN

Isaac Newton

tion of an inch of each other. The light from the two slits fell on a screen. Surprisingly he saw not just the simple accumulation of the light from both slits on the screen, but a pattern of light and dark lines.

He believed the pattern was the result of the mixing of the waves of light emanating from the respective slits.

At the time it was very difficult for the many justifiably avid fans of Isaac Newton to incorporate this new discovery into Newton's particle theory of light. Newton tried to explain optical phenomena such as refraction and reflection in terms of gravitational-like effects. As it turned out later, in a way, Newton's theory was given partial confirmation by the Quantum Theory.

The lines or "fringes" which Young saw, we call the interference pattern of the two light waves. When a crest interferes with a crest it is positive, or **constructive interference**, resulting in a bright spot. On the other hand, when a crest meets a trough we have a dark area or **destructive interference**.

As mentioned earlier, light waves oscillate at approximately 10^{15} Hz., or a million billion times per second. There is no machine known to man sensitive enough to record the individual fluctuations of the wave. We perceive the continuous additive effect of the light waves of which at each second 10^{15} wavelengths are interacting on the screen. This number, like so many numbers you may encounter in such fields as physics, astronomy and electronics, is incomprehensible. Yet precise measurement is part and parcel of the advance-

Albert Einstein

ment of science. Suffice it to say that one billion seconds, for example, equals roughly 30 years, and 10^{15} seconds is one million times that.

If the number is so fantastic and if even today we can't measure the waves individually, how did we discover that light was electromagnetic radiation? It's all thanks to the amazingly successful mathematical theory of J. Clark Maxwell, developed in 1864. He predicted not only the electromagnetic nature of light but also the speed at which it travels. Einstein used these same equations as a basis for his theory of special relativity. However, in order to understand exactly how light waves are formed, we had to wait until the year 1900 and the aforementioned Quantum Theory.

2. THE LASER

Now that we know a little something about light in general, we may consider the light source needed to perform holography: the laser, which stands for **light amplification by stimulated emission of radiation**. The understanding of the stimulated emission of light, or how a laser works, will greatly aid in conceptualizing the holographic process.

Without the laser, the unique three dimensional imaging characteristics and light phase recreation properties of holography would not exist as we know them today. Two years after the advent of the continuous wave laser, c. 1959-1960, Leith & Upatnieks (at the University of Michigan) reproduced Gabor's 1947 experiments with the laser, and launched modern holography.

A laser is a light amplifier, with very special characteristics. The laser was designed and made to work after two very useful theories had come on the scene. One is Niels Bohr's atomic theory and the other is the Quantum Theory. Niels Bohr, a Danish physicist, in the year 1913, proposed a model of the relationship between the electron and nucleus of the hydrogen atom. Bohr utilized the newly developed Quantum Theory in proposing that an electron circling the nucleus can assume certain discrete quantized levels of energy. In the lowest level, called the **ground state**, the electron is circling closest to the nucleus. However, if the atom is exposed to an outside source of energy the electron can be raised to a higher energy level, or an **excited state**, which is characterized by the electron carving a circle of greater circumference around the nucleus. It is important to note that the electron can't go just anywhere when it is excited but has to assume certain levels. Also, not just any energy would suffice in raising the electron's orbit. The energy must be equal to the energy difference between the ground state and the excited state the electron assumes. The frequency is the energy difference divided by "h" or Planck's constant. There are actually a number of different energy levels which the electron may assume but that is not essential to this explanation of how a laser works.

Energy is radiated in discrete packages, and these packages interact only on a very selective basis. There are two important reasons why lasers work. The laser depends on the very special emission character- istics of certain atoms whose electrons have been raised to the excited state. When the electron falls back down to its lower energy level (as all electrons eventually do), it in turn **emits** a package of electromagnetic or radiant **energy** which precisely equals the energy difference between the two levels, ground state and excited state. In a sense, what goes in comes out. This fact alone doesn't suffice in making a substance lase, for if too many electrons are in the ground state, the energy input would merely be absorbed by the electrons in the ground state which then might spontaneously emit a quantum of the correct size sometime in the future and that would be the end of that. We don't want to have an atom emitting its photon at just any old time, so we **stimulate** the atom to emit its energy package when we want it to. A package which would not be absorbed by another atom in ground state but would stimulate an atom already in an excited state to emit its own photon. In order to maintain the stimulated emission of photons which produce laser light, you must initiate and maintain a **population inversion.**

In lasers, electronic principles are applied to the visible portion of the spectrum. In electronics, oscillation is achieved with feedback around an amplifier. The feedback circuit determines the frequency of oscillation. In a laser, the tube of excited atoms is the amplifier. The mirror or resonator is the feedback circuit. Oscillation occurs at those wavelengths where the product of gain equals the loss, for a round trip, say starting from one mirror and coming back again. The gain of a laser is determined by population inversion, or having many more excited electrons, than

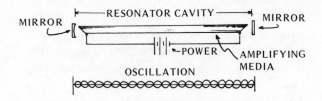

MIRROR — RESONATOR CAVITY — MIRROR

POWER — AMPLIFYING MEDIA

OSCILLATION

electrons in the ground state i.e. electrons. at their lowest energy level.

The helium-neon laser, which is probably the most common laser in use today (due to its relatively low cost) is the laser you will probably use most. The laser tube itself contains approximately 10% helium and 90% neon. Of these two inert gases, neon is the active agent in the lasing process. We could term helium the catalyst insofar as it facilitates the energy input to the neon. Before more energy is purposefully forced into the system, there is some action among the atoms and molecules comprising the gases. Some although very, very few of the electrons are already in the excited state, or upper energy levels and when they fall down, as they all tend to do, they emit a photon, only to be quickly absorbed.

The gain or loss of a photon or quantum of energy which is defined by a change in electron orbit takes place on the order of 10^{-8} seconds or 100 millionths of a second.

You might ask how even some of the atoms might have electrons in the excited state if there's no energy input, i.e., before the laser is switched on. The answer is purely statistical. For example, if you have a church filled to capacity for a Sunday morning mass, say 250 people, someone has got to cough or sneeze during the sermon. If you take the number of times some two or three people cough and compare that with the amount of times everyone in the church inhaled and exhaled without occasion, it would give you some idea of the situation in the laser tube before excitation. A few atoms are excited and then fall back to emit energy. This energy in turn goes off spontaneously to another atom whose electron almost certainly is in the ground state. The photon is absorbed. This is the key to the laser. If we have enough atoms with electrons in the **excited state**, the photon not only would not be absorbed, but when it did reach another excited atom it would induce it to cough up its own photon. We go from one, to two to four, to eight, to sixteen photons very rapidly. We have achieved **population inversion**, i.e., many more electrons are in the **excited state** than in the **ground state.**

Remember we are considering only the helium-neon laser. It is the most economical laser and probably the one you would be using. There are other lasers such as the argon-ion laser which is able to lase in both blue and green, and better yet a mixed gas argon-krypton ion laser which is able to lase in blue, green and red. The problem is that the prices of these lasers begin at around $6,000. If you have access to these lasers, you probably would not be reading this guide anyway.

There is also the pulse ruby laser which allows you to make holograms of animate objects. In the ruby laser chromium ions locked in a sapphire host are the sources of stimulated emission. The chromium atoms are excited by a light flash from a special flashlamp.

Let's backtrack slightly and talk briefly about the job helium performs before we go on to the more mechanical aspects of

Model KHC1 Mobile Holocamera

This is a picture of the basic components of a holographic camera manufactured by Korad.

Caution: The more powerful the laser the more care must be taken but as a rule, **never** look directly into the raw or unspread laser beam. The lens of your eye will focus the intense straight line laser light onto your retina causing lesions.

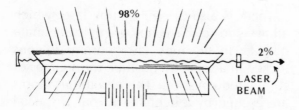

98%

2%

LASER
BEAM

laser operation. It so happens that helium has a metastable (or long lived) energy level that coincides quite well with one of the energy levels of neon which we need to obtain for lasing action to commence. Scientists discovered that it is much easier to raise helium to the excited state and let it transfer the correct energy packets to the neon when they meet inside the tube (which is at the correct pressure to assure their close acquaintance). So the helium is used as sort of a messenger, or filter, if you will, to store the correct high energy input originating from the laser power supply for the neon. Although the neon is the active ingredient in the laser, the helium greatly facilitates the process.

Virtually all we have so far, then, is a glorified light tube such as you might find lighting the streets of any late night hot spot worth its salt. The difference from this light tube stage of development to the functioning laser is essentially more of a mechanical characteristic, i.e., the precise geometrical relationship of its optical components.

The photons are emitted from the atoms inside the tube in all different directions. However, a very small percentage, around 2%, begin traveling in a horizontal direction within the tube. They naturally stimulate already excited atoms along the way to emit their photons in the same direction. This would actually mean nothing if we did not then place mirrors at both ends of the light tube in order to induce the light to start moving back and forth along the horizontal line of the tube. Eventually this induces a large number of photons to travel in the same direction and one of the mirrors is only partially reflective which lets the light leak out.

Some of the characteristics of laser light were introduced earlier. Now we should be able to discuss the properties of the laser with this further explanation: The source of the light is the energy given off when an atom's electron falls back down toward the ground state. There is only one type of atom taking part in the actual coherent, laser light giving process; therefore, according to the law of **Quantum Mechanics** the energy given off by identical energy shifts in each atom must be exactly the same. In other words each photon has precisely the same amount of energy. It will also have the same frequency and wavelength, and will be coherent light. It is the mirror set-up, sometimes called the **resonant cavity**, which induces this fully saturated, monochromatic light to exit the tube in a straight, narrow beam, for then not only do they contain the same amount of energy in stimulated emission, but the photons travel in the same direction.

Actually the precise wavelength emitted by a laser is determined by the mirror separation: The lasing transition gives a band of wavelengths over which the laser can emit.

The diameter of the exit beam varies with the bore of the tube but most helium neon beams are around 1.5mm diameter at exit and do not spread nearly as quickly as incoherent light would.

Thus laser light is coherent because it is radiated by a homogenous collection of atoms under precisely the same conditions. The mirrors at both ends make the small percentage of photons that hit the mirrors return in a straight line. This develops a cascade of light along the horizontal line of the tube. If you were to remove the laser casing you would see the same monochromatic, saturated light but the straight beam, so distinctive of laser light, would only be emitted from the end with the partially coated mirror. Now let's go on to see why we need these properties of coherent light and how we use them in holography.

3. THE BASIC HOLOGRAM

The hologram, that is, the medium which contains all the information, is nothing more than a high contrast, very fine grain, black and white photographic film. There are other photosensitive materials such as photo-chromic thermoplastics and ferro-electric crystals, but its very unlikely you will be working with these materials in the beginning, so, we will be dealing with silver halide emulsion much like the black and white film you can buy in your neighborhood drug store. Yet there is one very special difference; the film designed especially for holography is capable of very high resolution. One way of judging resolution of film or lenses is to see how many distinguishable lines can be resolved within a certain width, in this case it's a millimeter. Relatively slow film such as Kodak Pan X can resolve 90 lines per millimeter (depending on processing), while a good film designed for holography, such as AGFA Gaevert 8E75 is able to resolve up to 3000 lines/mm. Holographic film is also especially prepared to be sensitive to a certain wavelength of light and each type of film is given a code number — AGFA 8E75 is sensitive in the red region and thus is used with ruby or HeNe lasers; Kodak 649F is also, however, about 10 times slower. Kodak 120 plate or SO 173 film is very similar to AGFA 8E75 but not quite as sensitive.

Why the need for such special resolving power? The answer is that the hologram is not a recording of a focused image as in photography, but the recording of the interference of laser light waves that are bouncing off the object with another coherent laser beam, i.e., a reference beam which will be described later. The wavelengths of light from a HeNe laser are approximately 24 micro-inches or twenty-four millionths of an inch long, thus the need for such fine grain or high resolving power.

You will be able to understand the very important difference between holography and photography if we discuss simply what happens when you take a photograph and what happens when you make a hologram.

A **photograph** is basically the recording of the differing intensities of the light reflected by the object and imaged by a lens. The light is incoherent, therefore, there are many different wavelengths of light reflecting from the object and even the light of the same wavelength is out of phase. Your emulsion will react to the light image focused by the lens and the chemical change of the silver halide molecules will result from the photon bombardment. There is a point to point correspondence between the object and the emulsion. By this I mean that a point or collection of points which reflects light on your object, for example a white hat,

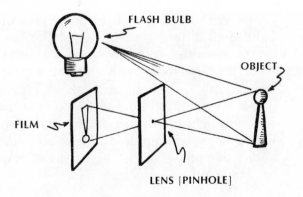

FLASH BULB

OBJECT

FILM

LENS [PINHOLE]

would be a source of more light to be focused by your lens than a black hat which would absorb rather than reflect light. The white object would expose more silver halide and after the development procedure, when you print your negative to make a positive on paper, less light from your enlarger bulb will be able to pass through that specific area in your negative and it will naturally be lighter in the positive.

Any object to be recorded can be thought of as the sum of billions of points on the object which are reflecting more or less light. The lens of the camera focuses each object point to a corresponding point on the film and there it exposes a proportional amount of silver halide. Thus, your record is of the intensity differences on the object which form a pattern that one may ultimately recognize as the object photographed. In holography we are working with light waves and with, most likely, a silver halide film, yet, beyond that it is very difficult to compare the two. As you well know by now the light sources are **vastly different**.

The sun or common light bulbs give off light of all different wavelengths. The laser emits a single wavelength of coherent light. If we were to simply illuminate our object with laser light and take a photograph, we would still only be recording the different light intensities of the object; we would not have captured any information about the phase of the light waves after bouncing off the object.

How can we capture this vital information? We need a standard or reference.

In the same way that a surveyor needs a reference point in order to make his measurements, we need a standard or a reference source in order to record the phase differences of the light waves and thus capture the information which supplies the vital dimensions and depth, to the holographic presentation. This standard we call a reference beam and it is supplied by the laser light itself.

The reference light is emitted in what we call a **plane** wave. By enlisting the aid of a beam splitter we are able to form two beams. The reference beam is allowed to hit the film directly. It might be spread with a lens and aimed at the film by a mirror, but for all practical purposes this does not affect the light waves.

The other beam which we will refer to as the **object** or **scene** beam is also usually spread by a lens and guided by a mirror but it is directed at the object being holographed.

Up until the instant in time that the object beam strikes the object, it too is a plane wave. As soon as it hits the object it is changed, or modulated according to the physical characteristics and dimensions of the object. So that the light which ultimately reaches the film plane after being reflected by the object now deviates in intensity and phase from the virtually unhampered reference beam. That difference is a function of the object. What once began as a plane wave is now bouncing off the object in a complex wavefront which consists of the summation of the multitude of infinitesmal object points reflecting light.

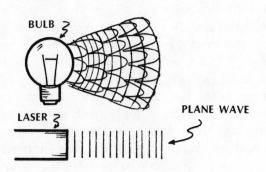

BULB

LASER

PLANE WAVE

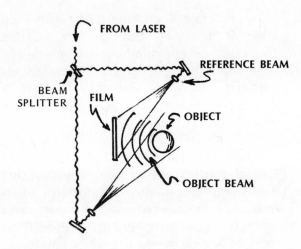

FROM LASER

REFERENCE BEAM

BEAM SPLITTER

FILM

OBJECT

OBJECT BEAM

WAVE FRONT

OBJECT

Using a laser in order to have this added information about the object would do us no good if the reference and object beams were not allowed to interfere at the film plane. The simplest interference that could take place on the film would be between the reference beam and the object beam but with no object at all. So that actually you have simply two plane waves coming from different directions and interfering on the film. Obviously in this case, it does not matter which you call the reference or object beam for neither carries any information about an object. And yet something very definitely is recorded. If we get a good understanding of this, the simplest case, it will be easier to understand as we move on to more complex situations.

The two beams are interfering with each other as they pass through one another. The crest of one plane wave meets the crest of another, or perhaps the crest meets a trough. This is reminiscent of the Thomas Young experiment on pages 5-6 but with much more coherent light.

When a crest meets a crest, it gives constructive interference and when a crest meets a trough, it gives destructive interference. Naturally where crest and crest meet there is more energy present and more of the atoms in the silver halide are affected or "exposed" than at a point on the film where a trough and crest meet. The accumulation of these points sets up a very fine stationary pattern or grating throughout space. The scheme of the pattern is a function of the wavelength of light, but more importantly, the angle difference between the two plane waves. We will get back to this point when we talk

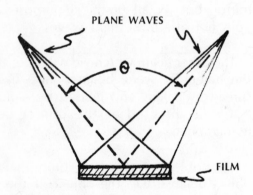

PLANE WAVES

θ

FILM

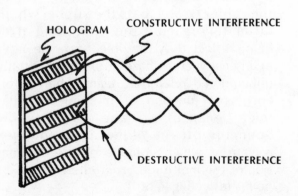

HOLOGRAM

CONSTRUCTIVE INTERFERENCE

DESTRUCTIVE INTERFERENCE

about the different types of holograms. It is important to remember that the direction of the light, phase of the light, etc., is preserved and coded in the emulsion by the very process of reference and object beam interference. So that if you were to shine number **one** beam back through the plate at the same angle you had in construction of the hologram, you would reconstruct the image of number **two** beam, and vice versa.

The very fine pattern which the emulsion assumes is a recording of the wavefronts as they interfere in the emulsion. It is definitely not a direct point to point recording of the image of the object but rather a recording of the interference between the coherent light that hit the object and that which did not.

We know that light, traveling in a wave form, can be bent or diffracted along its path of travel. One way to bend light is by the use of a lens. You may consider a hologram a very complex lens. It is bending and forming part of the light of the reference beam, which is used for reconstructing the image, into the wavefronts of the original object, so that you may perceive the object as if it were really there. All the infinitesimal little points that reflected light which interfered with the reference beam on the film are neatly focused to their respective positions in three dimensional space.

In most cases, the object will reconstruct its original size, regardless of the size of the plate, and the same distance from the film that it was when the hologram was made. The reference reconstruction beam will be focused by the complex hologram lens so that the front of the object appears closer, the back further away, and all the points in between are filled in accordingly. This might sound like a point to point correspondence very much like photography. However, there is a very special difference which makes holograms so wonderful.

I am sure that you have heard that if a hologram is broken or cut up, each small portion contains information about the whole object. This is because the light bouncing from each point on the object is not focused to a point on the film, but is allowed to spread out through space between the object and the film, thus covering a large portion of the film and interfering with the reference beam throughout that whole portion of the film as if each point were a spray of light each with a certain angle of divergence. So that every point is coded into a large area of the hologram. It might be easier to understand with this simple example. Let's say we have a very fine 11x14" hologram of a George Washington bust, complete with hat and plume. Two museums want this hologram (there is no other and the bust was destroyed in an earthquake) after much ado they decide to cut the hologram horizontally and exactly through the middle. Each museum then has a representation of the whole bust, unchanged in size but from different angles. It will be easier to understand this if you think of the hologram as a window into a room containing the bust. If the window is made smaller, the object does not shrink. We merely have a narrower angle of view of the object. You would be able to see, for

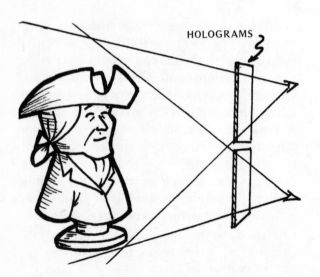

HOLOGRAMS

example, the plume, even from the bottom portion of the hologram; however, you may not be able to see the very tip top of the plume from the reconstructed angle of view of the lower part. This is because the light from that point was not able to spread enough to reach and interfere with the reference beam in the lower extremities of the plate. The holder of the upper portion would not get an especially good look under Washington's chin. One simple remedy would have been to move the object back from the plate and thus give the light more space in which to spread. However, as the object is placed farther back from the film it recedes from your personal three dimensional world.

4. MOVEMENT

One of the very prevalent practical problems in the making of a hologram is object movement. Unless you are lucky enough to own or have access to a pulsed ruby laser, you will have to look into the various methods of achieving object isolation. In the later section we will deal very specifically with the design and construction of isolation tables and optical mounts. I would like to spend a little time in this section trying to explain why we have to isolate the object from even the slightest movement in order to make a hologram.

If you are taking a photograph with relatively slow shutter speed, say 1/30th of a second, and your subject is moving rapidly across your line of sight, the photograph will be blurred. Sometimes this is done intentionally and with excellent results; but, for most photographers it means a ruined piece of film. In holography the slightest movement of the object does not blur the image but completely obliterates it. If you remember, we are not recording a focused image of the object but the interference of two wavefronts of light, the reference and object beams. The time needed to expose a hologram correctly is dependent on many things — the power of your laser, the sensitivity of your emulsion, and the reflectance of your object, among others. An average exposure for a common hologram is very roughly anywhere from a second to a minute. Let's say for the sake of argument that it is ten seconds. During those ten seconds the plane waves from the laser are being reflected and diffracted by the object. The resulting complex waves are then interfering with the reference beam in the emulsion. In essence you are recording interference fringes or patterns whose lines may only be separated by several wavelengths of light. This is an ongoing process taking place during the exposure. Remember when the laser beams are coherent, the interference pattern is stationary in space and thus can be recorded on film. If anything moves that is involved in this train of waves, by more than a fraction of a wavelength, the interference pattern will also move and the pattern is obliterated.

Any movement of the object, the film, or the optics caused by acoustic vibration, has the same fatal results. Obviously one way of reducing the chance of movement is by making the exposure very quick, say a billionth of a second, thus completely alleviating the need for isolation. Without the costly pulse ruby laser, you will need to construct an isolation table of relatively dense material and try to isolate all components from all sources of movement. For holograms which reconstruct an object clearly and brightly, all elements of your holographic set up should be stationary to less than $\lambda/10$, or one tenth of a wavelength of light.

5. DIFFERENT TYPES OF HOLOGRAMS

There are numerous types of holograms. It is important to learn the basic differences between the various types and what terms are used in referring to them so that you will understand immediately what someone means if he says, for example, he has just made a reflection hologram or transmission hologram or in line hologram. Holograms can differ in the way in which they are produced and they can differ in the way in which they incorporate and store the information for playback. The latter difference is the simplest to explain so we'll begin with that.

Under normal conditions we will be using a silver halide type film so we will talk about that specific case. The holographic information is coded in the emulsion according to the localized microscopic differences in the absorption of light or by the amount of silver halide converted to silver atoms during exposure and development. This is referred to as an **absorption** hologram. The absorption pattern on the film corresponds with the amount of light incident on the plate

Hologram Being Placed In Holder

during exposure. If that same hologram is put through a bleaching process it will then be termed a **phase hologram**. Bleaching is discussed in detail in chapter 10. The absorption index is converted to a refraction index by changing the different residues of silver to corresponding thicknesses of transparent substance. The hologram is then played back by the refraction of the reference beam dictated by changes of refraction in the emulsion. In a phase hologram the reference beam is phase modulated in order to reconstruct the wavefronts of the original objects. In absorption holograms the reference beam is diffracted by the small patterns of exposed emulsion in the form of silver residue.

Many holographers bleach all of their holograms because phase holograms absorb less valuable reconstructing laser light than the absorption type and thus create a brighter image. However, some holographers do not bleach regularly, especially if they have made a perfect exposure in their original hologram. This is due to the fact that there is a slight loss of resolution along with the gain in brightness. Also, a poor bleaching technique increases the amount of noise and can greatly reduce the resolution. The source of the controversy, if any, is merely personal taste.

It is important to remember that the term absorption or phase hologram has nothing to do with the way the hologram was exposed but, in the case of silver halide emulsion, refers only to a bleaching process which follows exposure and development, (although you may alter your development process if you know in advance you are going to bleach).

The following different types of holograms have special terms because they are actually **constructed** using different beam arrangements. Remember all the different types I'm about to describe can ultimately be either absorption or phase type holograms.

The inherent difference between holograms has caused scientists and holographers to develop special terms or adjectives for them. In the construction stage the difference is usually nothing more than the differing angle between the reference beam and object beam, as they interfere on the film. This angle difference can produce very pronounced differences between holograms in the playback stage. For example, a plane transmission hologram has to be reconstructed with laser light or a specially filtered light which approaches coherency in order for the reconstructed image to be crisp. A white light reflection hologram can in comparison be viewed quite clearly with sunlight or under ordinary incandescent light sources.

Very simply, as the angle difference between reference and object beam increases, the tiny patterns in the emulsion exposed by the crest-crest interference of light waves are set up closer and closer together. We'll discuss later the resulting properties of the varying distances between fringes, or the dark exposed areas in the hologram emulsion, but first let's get some terms straight.

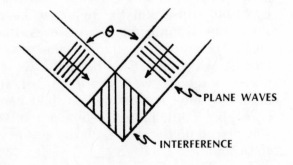

PLANE WAVES

INTERFERENCE

Dennis Gabor — Photo By Martha Holmes

The first hologram ever made by Dennis Gabor, in 1947, was an in-line, plane, transmission type. Remember at this time the laser was still yet to be developed, so Gabor had to make due with the quasi-coherent light gained by squeezing light from a mercury vapor lamp through a pinhole and then color filtering it (he used the 0.546 micron mercury green line). In-line means that the reference beam and object beam are coming from the same direction or are the same beam. Gabor had to do this in order to maintain the little coherency he had gained. All in-line holograms are also single beam set-ups. The same beam acts both as reference and object beam. This was made possible by using a transparency as the object. The light which went through the transparency before reaching the plate was modulated by the transparency, the light which went through it and was not effected by the transparency was the reference beam. The diffracted light and reference light interfered on the emulsion of the hologram and thus fulfilled one basic requirement for the construction of a hologram. When the reference beam was later shown back through the hologram at the same angle relationship it had with the plate in the reconstruction stage an image appeared. A poor image due to the lack of coherent light, but worse still the reference beam shone directly into the viewers eyes, thus greatly compromising the viewing of the reconstructed object. Although it was a poor image it was there in all its dimensionality. A new medium had been born, alas, a little prematurely and in 1948, was placed on the shelf until the advent of the laser.

Please note that through his experiments Gabor proved that an interference pattern carries all the information about the original object and that from the interference pattern one can reconstruct the object. For the discovery of these now well accepted concepts, Dennis Gabor received the 1971 Nobel Prize in Physics.

TRANSMISSION HOLOGRAMS

As I mentioned above in order to playback a hologram the reference beam must be shone back through the hologram at the same angle relationship as it had in construction. This is where the term transmission hologram arises. Transmission merely means that the reference beam must be transmitted through the hologram in order for the image to be reconstructed.

In 1962 Leith and Upatnieks at the University of Michigan removed Gabor's brain child from the shelf and gave holography its rebirth. Like Gabor they did their early experiments with a filtered mercury arc lamp. Leith and Upatnieks invented the off-axis reference beam with all its great advantages which they did not even appreciate at the time. After the development of the continuous wave gas laser in 1960 by Ali Javan et al. Leith and Upatnieks started using the laser and discovered the three dimensionality of the images. They performed these experiments as an adjunct to their work in side-looking microwave radar. They independently discovered off-axis holography only to find that Gabor had proposed holography 12-14 years earlier.

The term off-axis means that the reference beam and object beam are not coming from the same direction. Naturally in order to perform this feat we must have two different beams, thus the term twin beam. Because the laser gives a homogeneous beam of coherent light we can extract a beam from the original beam as I mentioned earlier. This is done with the aid of a beam splitter, which could be nothing more than a piece of optical glass. A part of the original beam goes through the glass and a part is reflected at the same angle as its incidence. This allows one to bring in the reference beam from an infinite number of angles in relation to the object directed beam, thus avoiding the inconvenience in play back of having to look directly into the reference beam as with the in-line, transmission hologram.

PLANE AND VOLUME HOLOGRAMS

This is a good time to point out the differences between a **plane** hologram and a **volume** hologram. As the angle difference between the object beam (or the wavefronts bouncing off the object) and the reference beam changes, so does the spacing of the patterns in the emulsion. As long as the angle difference remains less than 90° the hologram is called a plane hologram. Plane meaning that the holographic information is primarily contained in the two-dimensional plane of the emulsion. Although the emulsion does have a thickness, usually around seven microns or 7/millionths of a meter, the spacing between fringes is large enough, when the angle is under 90°, for us to imagine that the depth of the emulsion isn't really being utilized in the recording of the hologram. At 90°, which is really a convenient but arbitrary point, the angle is great enough and the fringe spacing has become small enough for us to say that the recording process is taking place throughout the volume of thickness of the emulsion. A point to remember is that although there are different thicknesses of emulsion put on celluloid or glass plates seven microns is an average. One can use the same emulsion say seven microns thick, and make both plane and volume holograms depending on the angle difference between reference and object beam.

Thus if you imagine your film in a fixed plane and your object in a stationary position, as you rotate the incidence angle of the reference beam, you can determine whether you are making a plane or volume hologram. If your angle is under 90° its plane, from 90° – 180° it's volume. Naturally, past 180° you merely begin coming back the other way, through the volume to the plane and when finally you reach 360° you are back at the in-line, plane, transmission hologram and you can collect your $200.

A very important point for a differentiation occurs as the reference beam swings around its arc of possible positions. In a **plane transmission** hologram the reference beam is hitting the film from the same side as the object beam. In a **volume reflection** hologram the reference beam has made an arc clear around so that it hits the film from the opposite side as the modulated object beam. When 180° difference is reached you are then constructing an **in-line**, **volume**, **reflection hologram**. The fringes become so tightly spaced that the distance between them is half of a wavelength of light. This is the angle difference which gives the least distance between fringes.

POSSIBLE REFERENCE BEAM ANGLES

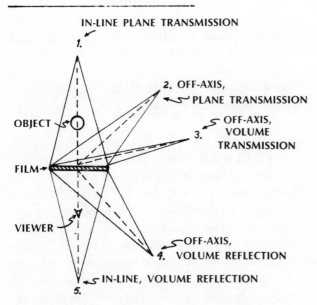

IN-LINE PLANE TRANSMISSION
1.
2. OFF-AXIS, PLANE TRANSMISSION
3. OFF-AXIS, VOLUME TRANSMISSION
OBJECT
FILM
VIEWER
4. OFF-AXIS, VOLUME REFLECTION
5. IN-LINE, VOLUME REFLECTION

Ponder the possibilities of magnification if one were able to make a hologram with x-rays or cosmic rays and then play back with low frequency visible light. Needless to say, there are a few problems that need to be licked before this can be realized; however the possibilities in themselves are exciting particularly when we remember that x-ray wavelengths are smaller than atoms.

A transmission type hologram means that the reference beam must be transmitted through the hologram, in order to decode the interference patterns and render the reconstructed image. The light which is used for playback must be coherent or semi-coherent or the image will not be sharp. If a non-coherent source, such as the light from a common, unfiltered slide projector is used, then the hologram will diffract all the different wavelengths. The interference pattern or grating etched in the emulsion is not particular as to which wavelengths it bends or focuses; therefore, you end up with an unclear overlapping spectrum of colors which somewhat resemble your object.

A hologram will playback just as well with laser light of a different color or wavelength than the light with which it was made. However, the object will appear to be of a different size and/or distance from the plate. For example, a hologram of an object made with neon or red light will playback that object smaller or seemingly further away if a blue color laser is used. This is because the grating will bend the blue or shorter light less severely than the red with which it was made and with which it is meant to be decoded.

REFLECTION HOLOGRAM

Unlike a plane hologram, sometimes called a thin hologram, which requires a coherent or highly filtered playback source, a **reflection**, or **thick**, **hologram** can be viewed very satisfactorily in white light or light which contains many different wavelengths. The one requisite is that the light be from a point source and be a somewhat straight line, such as a slide projector light or penlight, or the sun on a clear day. The reflection hologram can do this because in a way it acts as its own filter.

In a reflection hologram the fringes are packed so closely together that they constitute layers throughout the thickness of the emulsion. The spacing between fringes remains constant. If "d" or the distance between fringe one and two is two microns for example, then the distance between the remaining layers of fringes will also be two microns. This distance is a function of the wavelength of light used in constructing the hologram and also the angle difference between reference and object beam. This layered affair allows the reflection hologram to absorb, or not reflect, any of the colors or wavelengths of light which are not the correct length. The wavelength which matches the fringe spacing will be reflected: the crests of the wavelengths which are too short or too long will eventually miss one of the planes and be absorbed into the darkness of the emulsion.

In a reflection type hologram the playback light or reconstruction beam comes from the same side of the hologram as the viewer. Some parts of the incident light are reflected, some are not, depending on the interference pattern. If the hologram was made correctly the result should be a visible three dimensional image. As I mentioned before in the transmission type the reconstruction beam must pass through the hologram and come towards the viewer from the opposite side of the hologram while in the reflection type the playback source comes from the same side of the hologram as the viewer.

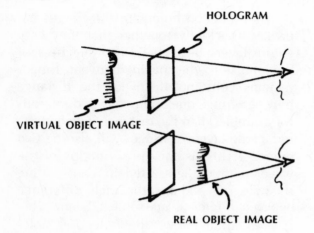

HOLOGRAM

VIRTUAL OBJECT IMAGE

REAL OBJECT IMAGE

Incidentally just as very few transmission holograms are made in-line or 0° so are very few reflection holograms made in-line or else you would have to hold your point light source in your teeth or perhaps invest in a miner's cap. Most reflection holograms are made at a less severe angle, perhaps 160°, so that the light can come in at an angle without being blocked by the person who is trying to see the hologram.

The image produced by the hologram can either appear to be in front of the holographic plate or film, or behind the film. In the former case it is called a **real** image (projection) and the latter a **virtual** image. If you imagine your position as viewer to be constant then you can easily determine whether an image is real or virtual. If the image appears between you and the hologram it is a real image, if the hologram is between you and the apparent object then it is called a virtual image. In general it is easier to view a virtual image because you can see through the hologram as if it were a window. You are confined in your view to the object by the size of the window. I would like to mention here that as with other windows if you change the size of the window the object or objects you are viewing do not change their size. For example, let's say you are lucky enough to have a window in your house that looks out on a beautiful tree. If for some terrible reason you have to make your window smaller, your tree luckily does not shrink, you merely have a more confined view or less possible angles of view of the tree.

To view a virtual image you must look through the hologram to perceive the object floating in the space behind it. In order to see a real image you look at the hologram and see the object in free space in front of the hologram. It is a little more difficult to view a real image because you have to find the image or focus your eyes in front of the hologram and in this case the hologram is less capable to act as a guide for your eyes. You may move a screen or sheet of paper back and forth in front of the hologram in order to find where the object is focused and then, keeping your eye on that place in space, remove the sheet and look straight into the hologram.

The real image is very exciting but there are a number of drawbacks. The object holographed should be quite a bit smaller than the size of the film you are using, if not, you will not be able to see the complete real image of the object all at once. It will necessitate craning your neck and stretching in all which ways to see parts of the whole object or objects. Also, unless you take special precautions in the construction of the hologram, the real image will be pseudoscopic. This means simply that everything that was closer to the film when the hologram was made will now be further away and vice versa. This includes both individual objects in a shot or the different planes of space of an individual object. The pseudoscopic image is made by reversing the direction of the reference beam, or by turning the completed hologram around until seeing the image in front of the plate.

For example, if in making your hologram you placed a salt shaker closer to the film than a pepper shaker (let's imagine the salt shaker is even casting a shadow from the object beam onto the pepper shaker), then

ORTHOSCOPIC   PSEUDOSCOPIC

SHADOW   HOLOGRAM   SHADOW

PEPPER   SALT   SALT   PEPPER

in a pseudoscopic playback as a real image the pepper shaker will appear to be closer to you than the salt shaker. But very curiously indeed, the pepper shaker still has the shadow from the salt shaker which is no longer there.

Naturally, if you playback the virtual image of the same hologram the shakers would resume their original positions (in the latter sections we will discuss further the real image hologram, show possible ways of making holograms specifically for real image playback and also touch lightly on why there is a real image.)

In addition to the previously mentioned types of holograms commonly made today there is the multiplex hologram and the image hologram (see page 35). These types of holograms are being used more commonly today.

Very simply the multiplex hologram is the holographic storage of photographic information. In the first stage a series of photographs or a certain amount of motion picture footage of the subject is exposed. The number of stills or frames taken depends on how much of an angle of view you want of the subject in your finished hologram. For example if you want a 360° view of the subject (see page 37) you might expose 3 frames per degree of movement around the subject (usually the camera remains stationary and the subject rotates) this will result in the exposure of 1080 frames. When your film is developed you proceed to the holographic lab and (using a laser) make a series of "slit" holograms using each frame of film as a subject for each slit of holographic film. The silts are usually about one millimeter wide and are packed so closely that there is no "dead space" in between. Also the hologram is bleached so that the strips disappear. Usually a multiplex hologram yields **horizontal** not vertical parallax. This is because the camera usually moves **around** (or the subject moves **around** in front of the camera) and doesn't usually pass **over** the subject. Also, psychologically, horizontal parallax is much more desirable and the lack of horizontal parallax, to humans, is much more noticeable than the lack of vertical parallax. The multiplex hologram is usually, though not always, made on flexible film coated with the same holographic emulsion as the plates. The procedure can be totally mechanized so that a machine can expose a slit hologram per each frame of footage at a very rapid pace. The advantage of this type of hologram is that you can now have a hologram of almost anything you can capture on ordinary film without the need of the expensive, clumsy pulse ruby laser. The disadvantage is that it is not truly a hologram but photographic information holographically stored. It seems that it will have a very solid place in the growing field of display and advertising holography.

NOTE

For further information please refer to: T. Kashara, Y. Kimura and M. Kawai "3-D construction of imaginary objects by the method of holographic stereogram" in *Applications of Holography*, E. V. Barrekette et. al. eds. (Plenum Press, N.Y., 1969) pp. 19-34 Lloyd Cross, mentioned in the back of the book, under Schools, is an expert on multiplex holography.

The image hologram which was mentioned earlier also has an advantage which will make it one of the types widely used in display holography. The image hologram can be played back with ordinary "white light" from an uncoated incandescent bulb. An image hologram can be either reflection type or transmission type however, it is more impressive as a transmission type because unlike an ordinary transmis-

NOTE

Please keep in mind that not all image Transmission holograms are of the type that can playback with ordinary light. In order to achieve this, a narrow strip of laser light is made by the use of a cylindrical lens to reduce the image parallax. There is as yet no commonly accepted name for a hologram made in this fashion. Although they are sometimes called "rainbow" or "spectral" holograms they are not true holograms because they have forfeited one axis of parallax (usually the vertical) as in the multiplex type hologram. The image produced by a "rainbow" or "spectral" hologram is also slightly harder to view than that produced by an ordinary hologram. For an excellent discussion of these types of holograms and for an excellent review of display holography we suggest you read: "Holographic Displays — A Review" by Stephen A. Benton in *Optical Engineering* Sept.-Oct. 1975.

6. COHERENCE LENGTH

sion hologram the image transmission hologram can play back well with an unfiltered white light source. The image hologram can be formed by placing the correct lens between the subject or scene and the holographic film plane. The subject is thusly focused directly onto the film plane and a hologram is made of that focused image. This type of hologram is very pleasing because the object seems to come out at you like a **real image** but it is not pseudoscopic. The real advantage is that the image transmission hologram has much less color dispersion or spectral smear than an ordinary transmission hologram and when you playback with an ordinary uncoated light bulb there is a rainbow effect but the image remains very sharp. Another way to make an image hologram is by copying the focused real pseudoscopic image of an original or master hologram. The result is a second generation image transmission hologram whose virtual image is orthoscopic.

Every laser has what is termed a coherence length. It is related to the length of the laser tube and the purity of the phase of light emitted and the wavelength itself. The more pure the light the greater the coherence length. That is, not just any kind of laser can be used in making a hologram. On the specification sheets of most high quality lasers manufactured today you will see the term TEM ∞. This means that the laser is operating in the lowest transverse mode, which is the most uniform across the beam and is preferred for holography. A laser intended for making holograms must ideally be lasing in just

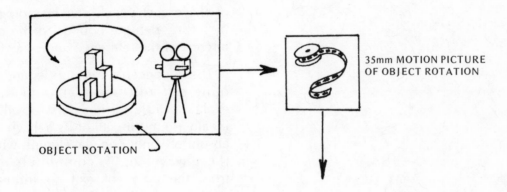

35mm MOTION PICTURE
OF OBJECT ROTATION

OBJECT ROTATION

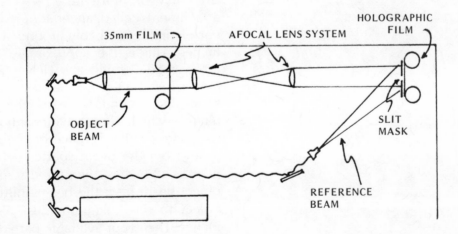

HOLOGRAPHIC
FILM

35mm FILM

AFOCAL LENS SYSTEM

OBJECT
BEAM

SLIT
MASK

REFERENCE
BEAM

(coherence continued)

one longitudinal mode. Both of these qualifications, i.e. spatial coherence and longitudinal coherence, define the purity of the light.

In twin beam holography it is extremely important to measure the paths of the reference beam and object beam(s) for even if you are using the prescribed laser for holography its coherence length is not infinite. The coherence length also places an upper limit on the size, especially depth, of the object which can be holographed by setting definite bounds to the path difference of the reference and object beams.

These concepts are subtle and can be quite difficult to understand so let me explain a little further. First of all, a laser ideally is emitting all of its light in one and absolutely only one wavelength with all of those wavelengths completely in phase from the point of exit to infinity. This would be wonderful, but unless you have a fifty mW or more laser with a special attachment called an etalon, your coherence length is probably around six to eight inches. This is the approximate length of an average 5 milliwatt, HeNe laser. This means that once you separate your original beam and secondary beam, the path difference which they travel cannot exceed six inches. If the distance of the reference beam from the beam splitter to the hologram is 48 inches, then the distance of the object beam from the beam splitter to the object to the hologram must also be 48 inches. Then your available path difference can be utilized totally by your object.

In a way this can be related to depth of field in photography, but in holography outside of that depth of six inches the object drops off into nothingness. In a way, you "focus" on your object by making sure the lengths of your object beam(s) and reference beam are measured correctly.

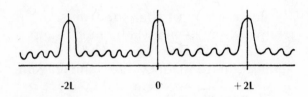

-2L   0   + 2L

NOTE

The coherence length is vitally affected by the type of laser used. Depending on the kind of laser you are working with you may have to adjust the length (the difference can be sizable). When in doubt check with the manufacturer.

The light being emitted by lasers has what you might call a coherence curve. It is a bell shaped curve which shows, in distance from the exit point of the laser, where the wavelengths are most in phase. This is usually a constant integer and depends on the wavelength or substance which is lasing, the size of the laser as well as how purely it is emitted. This number, let's say eight inches, remains constant. At the peak of the curve, or every eight inches, the light is most in phase. You would make the path lengths of your beams multiples of twice the cavity length of your laser. In addition, the coherence function repeats itself. It is at maximum again at a distance of twice the mirror separation in the laser. It repeats itself every 2L distance.

Before buying a laser for use in holography it is always wise to inquire about all the pertinent characteristics of its functions.

We will spend more time in later sections on coherence length, on reference and object beam intensity ratios and all the practical information one needs in order to perform holography. At this point, however, we feel you have been offered enough of the basic theory of holography and now we will begin applying all of this to the construction of a lab and construction of holograms. Naturally as your practical experience grows you will be able to absorb more theory, but now let's start with the isolation table, or in more colloquial terms, from the ground up.

7. CONSTRUCTION OF A LABORATORY SET-UP

Basic Holographic Equipment

ISOLATION TABLE

Construction of the isolation table is relatively simple and will be much simpler if you have the ¾" plywood and the 4x10" lumber cut to size by the lumber yard.

The roofing tar is used to fill in any air spaces that may occur between joints, thus making a completely solid unit. The tar can be purchased at a hardware store by the gallon.

Obtain the inner tube from a tire store and the sheet metal from a sheet metal fabrication company (look in the Yellow Pages).

LIST OF MATERIALS:

> Quantity: 5-doz. 2" #8 flat head wood screws
> 5-doz. ½" #8 flat head wood screws
> 1-gal. roofing tar
> 1-#1020 inner tube
> 1-4' x 4' 8-gage sheet metal
> 3-¾" x 4' x 4' interior plywood
> 4-4" x 10" x 4' lumber
> 2-cans flat black spray paint

This table, suspended on the inner tube, is an air flotation system that will settle out vibrations rapidly and can be used successfully in isolating an object and optical components from vibrations up to half the wavelength of 6328Å light.

ISOLATION TABLE

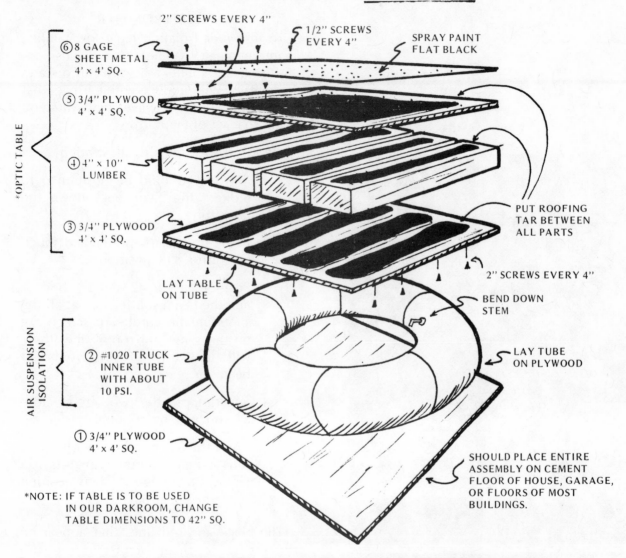

2" SCREWS EVERY 4"

1/2" SCREWS EVERY 4"

SPRAY PAINT FLAT BLACK

⑥ 8 GAGE SHEET METAL 4' x 4' SQ.

⑤ 3/4" PLYWOOD 4' x 4' SQ.

*OPTIC TABLE

④ 4" x 10" LUMBER

③ 3/4" PLYWOOD 4' x 4' SQ.

PUT ROOFING TAR BETWEEN ALL PARTS

2" SCREWS EVERY 4"

LAY TABLE ON TUBE

BEND DOWN STEM

AIR SUSPENSION ISOLATION

② #1020 TRUCK INNER TUBE WITH ABOUT 10 PSI.

LAY TUBE ON PLYWOOD

① 3/4" PLYWOOD 4' x 4' SQ.

SHOULD PLACE ENTIRE ASSEMBLY ON CEMENT FLOOR OF HOUSE, GARAGE, OR FLOORS OF MOST BUILDINGS.

*NOTE: IF TABLE IS TO BE USED IN OUR DARKROOM, CHANGE TABLE DIMENSIONS TO 42" SQ.

NOTE

It is important that your isolation table be placed on a solid floor, such as a cement slab in a garage. Wooded floors are not recommended. If your table is not quite stable enough after testing it with the interferometer set-up described in the next section, try putting a 3" level of newspaper under the whole table as a primary cushion. Or try putting it on a table with legs in buckets of sand.

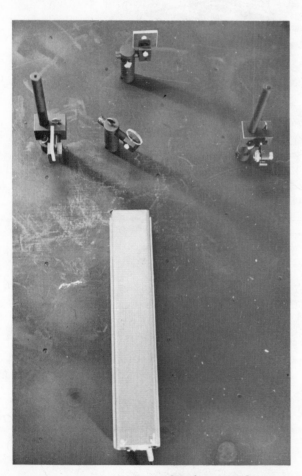

Interferometer Set-up

INTERFEROMETER

To test your isolation table for stability, an interferometer can be set-up. By positioning the beam splitter, the two mirrors and the lens you will produce visible fringes that show a fraction of a wavelength variation in the spacing of the mirrors.

PROCEDURE: (refer to illustration)

1. Mirror #1 should be positioned to redirect the beam back down the laser tube.

2. Insert the beam splitter and touch up mirror #1's position.

3. Position mirror #2 and tilt both it and the beam splitter so that all the spots on the cardboard screen are on the same horizontal line (there will be two sets with two bright beams in each set).

4. Superimpose the two sets as close as you can by rotating mirror #2.

5. Insert the 60x microscope objective lens (see note in Transmission Hologram section for lens position technique page 51).

The black and red lines that appear on the screen represent constructive and destructive interference between the two plane waves from the two mirrors. These are the types of interference that must be recorded to produce a hologram.

Walk on the floor, stamp on it, yell, sneeze, clap your hands over the table; these vibrations will probably cause the fringes to blur. If the fringes blur during exposure of the film, you will not get a hologram. If they blur part way through the exposure, you will get a hologram. However, the image will have very little contrast because only part of the exposed information is interference, the rest is just light exposure with no information.

You may notice that the center fringe pattern appears to "breathe." This is all right and is caused by changes in air pressure over the table.

You have now assured yourself of the **most** important consideration in holography: **STABILITY**.

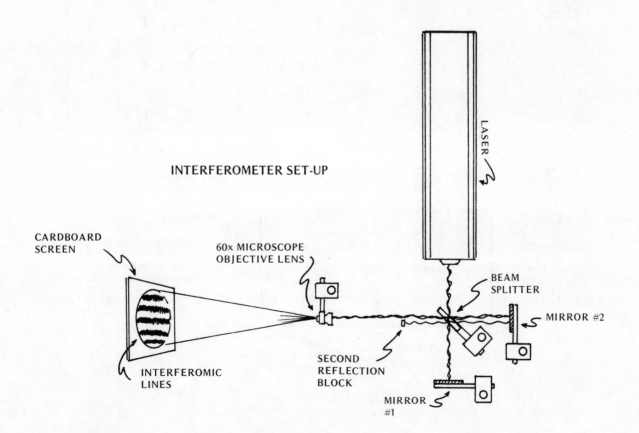

INTERFEROMETER SET-UP

CARDBOARD SCREEN

60x MICROSCOPE OBJECTIVE LENS

LASER

BEAM SPLITTER

MIRROR #2

INTERFEROMIC LINES

SECOND REFLECTION BLOCK

MIRROR #1

DARKROOM CONSTRUCTION

For those of you who do not have a suitable space to use as a darkroom, we have this example of a 4 x8 ′ darkroom.

If construction is not possible an alternate could be to sew strips of black plastic that can be bought by the yard from a large fabric store and hang them from the ceiling. This type of darkroom could only be used in the evening or in a **very** dimly lit area because of the light leakage problem.

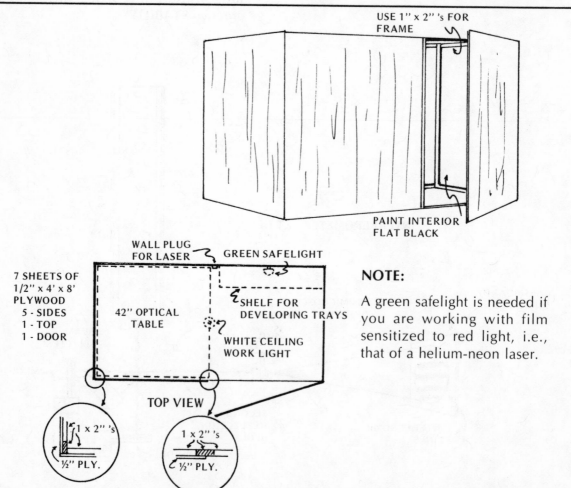

USE 1" x 2" 's FOR FRAME

PAINT INTERIOR FLAT BLACK

WALL PLUG FOR LASER   GREEN SAFELIGHT

7 SHEETS OF 1/2" x 4' x 8' PLYWOOD
5 - SIDES
1 - TOP
1 - DOOR

42" OPTICAL TABLE

SHELF FOR DEVELOPING TRAYS

WHITE CEILING WORK LIGHT

TOP VIEW

1 x 2" 's
½" PLY.

1 x 2" 's
½" PLY.

NOTE:

A green safelight is needed if you are working with film sensitized to red light, i.e., that of a helium-neon laser.

OPTICS AND OPTICAL MOUNTS

Here are the minimum optics necessary for making Transmission and Reflection holograms and the interferometer test set up. The list of suppliers contains the names of manufacturers and distributors of optics in various sizes and types that you may want or need to make other set ups.

Quantity: 3-2 x 2" front Surface Mirrors (Edmund #40, 040 51 x 76 mms. at $1 ea.)*

1-2 x 2" Flat Glass for Beam Splitter (Edmund #2269 52 x 113 mms. at $.75 ea.)*

2-60x Microscope Objective Lenses (Edmund #30, 049 at $30 ea.)*

* Prices subject to change

Two pieces of ground glass, spaced 10 cm. apart, can be used as an object beam spreader, therefore eliminating one objective lense. This eliminates lens cleaning and beam alignment problems, and is less expensive. If you use a lens you should take the lenses apart and use only the final, very small lens to spread the beam.

Because of the high cost of optical mounts made especially for holography, we have over the past ten years fabricated all our own optical mounts. These mounts have all the stability and versatility of mounts that are produced today costing 10 times as much.

Mirrors And Spreading Lenses

All our mounts (refer to illustration on next page) are made from heavy aluminum stock available at surplus stores (check your Yellow Pages under Metals or Aluminum); these places will usually cut the aluminum to size. The large holes can be drilled by a machine shop leaving the small drilling, tapping, and end filing to you. To keep reflections down, it is best to spray paint everything flat black. Epoxy everything together with the new 10 second epoxy that is now available from hardware stores. Aircraft surplus has the nylon screws.

Optical Mount

The quantity indicated in the illustration is for the minimum number needed. You will probably want to make or order different kinds for various other experiments.

Some mounts can be made from wood, however, remember that stability is a prime ingredient of successful holography.

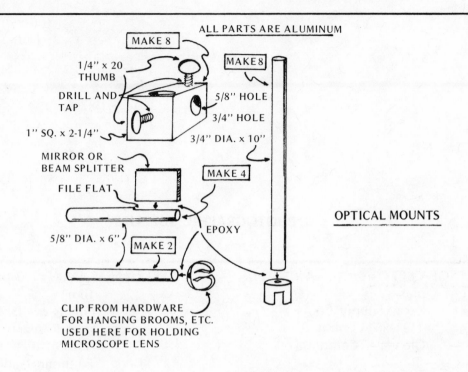

ALL PARTS ARE ALUMINUM

MAKE 8

1/4" x 20 THUMB

MAKE 8

DRILL AND TAP

5/8" HOLE

3/4" HOLE

1" SQ. x 2-1/4"

3/4" DIA. x 10"

MIRROR OR BEAM SPLITTER

MAKE 4

FILE FLAT

OPTICAL MOUNTS

5/8" DIA. x 6"

MAKE 2

EPOXY

CLIP FROM HARDWARE FOR HANGING BROOMS, ETC. USED HERE FOR HOLDING MICROSCOPE LENS

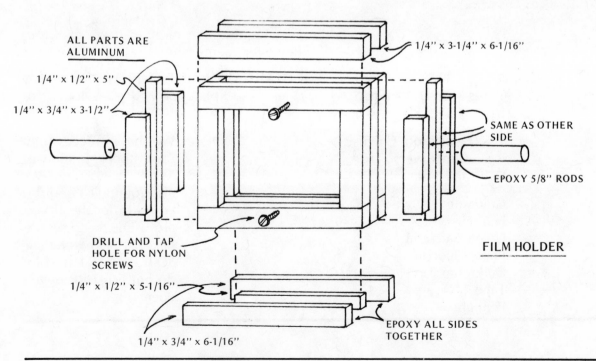

ALL PARTS ARE ALUMINUM

1/4" x 3-1/4" x 6-1/16"

1/4" x 1/2" x 5"

1/4" x 3/4" x 3-1/2"

SAME AS OTHER SIDE

EPOXY 5/8" RODS

DRILL AND TAP HOLE FOR NYLON SCREWS

FILM HOLDER

1/4" x 1/2" x 5-1/16"

1/4" x 3/4" x 6-1/16"

EPOXY ALL SIDES TOGETHER

PHOTOGRAPHIC SUPPLIES

FILM: AGFA 8E75 nonAh (4 x 5″ glass plates)
X-Ray Supply Co.
1121 So. Central
Glendale, California

EASTMAN KODAK #120 plates or SO 173 film
Film is available through Newport Research Corp.
18235 Mt. Baldy Circle
Fountain Valley, Ca. 92708

SUPPLIES: Quan. 4 — 8 x 10″ Photo Trays (for D-19, Stop Bath, Fixer, Photo-Flo)

2 — 1 gal. Photo Chemical Containers (for D-19 and Fixer)

Graduate
Funnel
Green Safelight
Photo Sponge
Darkroom Timer
Tape Measure
Penlight

CHEMICALS: Kodak D-19 for Kodak 120 plate or HRP Developer for AGFA 8E75 plate.

Note: We have successfully used Kodak D-19 with AGFA 8E75 film. We also found D-19 a little easier to locate. If you are using the new Kodak 120 plates or their SO173 ESTAR base film **do not** use HRP developer.

LIGHT METER

Part of your holographic set-up requires a very sensitive light meter. The light level of a low power, spread laser beam is not enough to activate a conventional light meter, hence, we have developed a simple, accurate "Light Meter", a Triplet V-O-M Meter with a Cadmium Sulfide photo cell obtained from most electronic supply stores.

To use, first attach the photocell wires to the meter leads and plug the leads into the "COM" and "V-O-M" receptors. There are no polarity requirements, so either wire can go to either lead and either lead to either receptor.

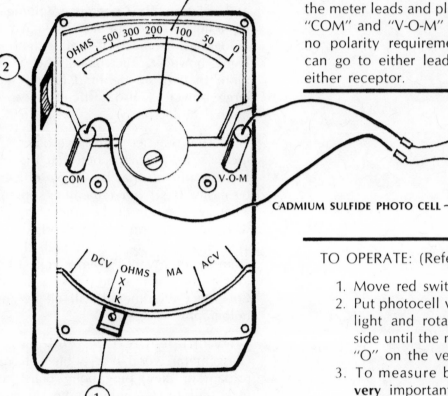

CADMIUM SULFIDE PHOTO CELL

TRIPLET MODEL 310 V-O-M METER

TO OPERATE: (Refer to illustration)

1. Move red switch to **X1K OHMS**.
2. Put photocell very close to a bright light and rotate the knob on the side until the needle is right on the "O" on the very top scale.
3. To measure beam intensity it is **very** important to remember that the meter's scale will read in such a way that the **BRIGHTER** the light falling on the photocell the **LOWER** the number on the scale.

> Example: A reading of "50" is twice as bright as a reading of "100".

8. MAKING HOLOGRAMS

OBJECTS

In most holograms the object is displayed against black space, therefore, the hologram looks best with white or very light colored objects. Using a securely mounted piece of wood painted white makes a good white background to display dark objects. Don't forget to place it within the Coherence Volume or it will not appear in the hologram.

Object size is dependent upon depth and isolation. The Coherence Volume of 6" has a height of several feet. We have made holograms of objects 18" tall with no problems, however, the objects were never more than 6" in depth. Lighting such a large object is also difficult because of limited table space.

A usual practice with large objects is to increase the distance between the object and the film so that the whole object can be easily seen; but remember, no matter what size the film or the object, the object will always reconstruct its original size. You may have to look through the hologram at some very extreme angles, but as long as the object is properly lit and in the Coherence Volume, it will all be in the holographic image.

Try different textures and materials. Glass, metal, wood, ivory, objects from styrofoam or clay, ping pong balls, toothpick sculpture, anything. We do suggest that you use objects which reflect a good amount of light.

Be careful of materials which are **highly** reflective because the meter reading may be deceptive when it reads those highlights that are direct light reflections back to the film plane. You might want to spray on dulling spray that can be obtained from a photographic supply store.

Try putting a magnifying glass or a mirror in with the object. Some surprising optical illusions can be created.

The most important thing to remember when choosing an object is **stability**.

BASIC TRANSMISSION HOLOGRAM

We use the word "Basic" because there are as many different configurations as there are holographers. Below is a beginning set up and in a later section we will show you others that are used for different reasons.

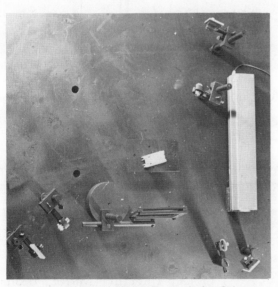

Basic Transmission Set-up

NOTE: As you can see in the illustration the components are placed with specific measurements. This is because of the coherence length of 6328Å light. It is a good rule of thumb to have the final distance from the first beam splitter through the set up to the film be a multiple of twice the length of your laser cavity.

NOTE: The Coherence Volume is roughly 6" in depth, meaning that any object placed within this space will make a hologram — outside this area the object is too far out of phase with the reference beam.

TRANSMISSION SET-UP

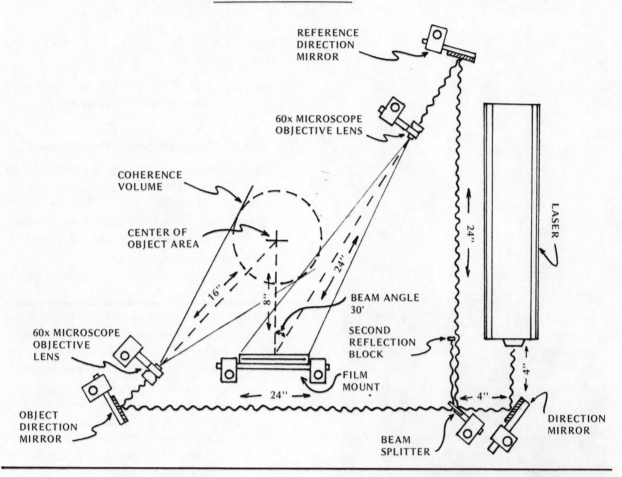

REFERENCE DIRECTION MIRROR

60x MICROSCOPE OBJECTIVE LENS

COHERENCE VOLUME

CENTER OF OBJECT AREA

16"

8"

24"

BEAM ANGLE 30°

SECOND REFLECTION BLOCK

FILM MOUNT

24"

LASER

24"

4"

4"

60x MICROSCOPE OBJECTIVE LENS

OBJECT DIRECTION MIRROR

BEAM SPLITTER

DIRECTION MIRROR

TO SET UP (Refer to illustration)

CHECKLIST

1. Place the Laser, Direction Mirror, Object Direction Mirror, Beam Splitter, Reference Direction Mirror, and the Film Holder in their approximate positions. The Film Holder should have the thumb screws on the opposite side from the object area.

2. Measure these components for proper placement using a piece of tape for the Center of Object Area. Both the reference beam path and the object beam path must be of equal length from the Beam Splitter through the set up to the film. In the illustration 48″ is used.

3. Turn on the Laser and adjust components for beam landing. Put a piece of white cardboard in the Film Holder for reference beam landing — it should hit the center of the cardboard.

4. You will notice two beams reflecting off the Beam Splitter. These are first and second reflections. Use a piece of black cardboard to block the second reflection.

5. Position 60x Lens in the reference beam.

NOTE

It can be difficult directing a 1.5mm beam through a 2mm diameter lens. First lower the lens and adjust the mount so that the beam glides across the top of the lens holder in the direction of the lens. Then carefully raise the lens until you see the spread beam exit. Adjust the lens so that the beam fills the cardboard in the Film Holder. You may notice concentric rings on the cardboard. These are either imperfections in the lens or dust on the lens. Try cleaning with lens tissue. If rings still exist, carefully rotate the lens in its holder to put the rings off the cardboard.

6. Place the object so that it is in the center of the Coherence Volume. Solid white objects about as big as your fist work best for beginning holograms. We will discuss other types of objects later.

7. Position the other 60x Lens or pair of ground glass diffusers in the object beam with the same technique as in the note under step 5. The spread beam may not completely light the object. This may mean that you will have to place the lens before the Object Direction Mirror instead of after it as in the illustration. Look through the Film Holder, rotate the object until you like the composition, and secure the object to the table with a drop of 10 second epoxy or non-hardening clay. It will take a few minutes for the epoxy and clay to solidify.

8. Measuring the beam intensity ratios is most important to insure good contrast in the final image. Take the Light Meter and make the necessary preparations as described in the Light Meter section. The optimum beam ratio is between 2:1 to 5:1 — The reference beam should be 2X to 5X brighter than the light reflecting from the object toward the film plate.

9. Put a piece of black cardboard in front of the Laser to use as a shutter.

TO MEASURE

1. Turn the lights off.
2. Block the object beam with a piece of black cardboard somewhere between the Beam Splitter and the Object Direction Mirror.
3. Put the photocell against the cardboard in the Film Holder tilted toward the reference beam coming from the lens.
4. Read the meter's top scale (you can use a penlight).
5. Block the reference beam with cardboard somewhere between the Beam Splitter and the Reference Direction Mirror.

6. Put the photocell flat against the cardboard in the Film Holder facing the object.

7. Read the meter's scale.

Remember that the meter reads backwards. The **Brighter** the beam the **Lower** the number.

8. If ratios are over 5:1 or under 2:1, move the object lens closer or farther from the object and/or move the reference lens closer or farther from the Film Holder. Check to be sure that the object and film are still completely lit.

10. In the dark with only the safe light on, insert the film into the Film Holder with the emulsion facing the object, gently tighten the nylon screws, and step back for a minute to let the table stop moving and allow the air to settle.

You can tell which side the emulsion is on by lightly wetting your lips and touching the film between them for a few seconds. As you part your lips one side will stick — that is the emulsion side.

11. Gently pick up the black cardboard shutter and suspend it directly in front of the laser beam for a mental count of 10.

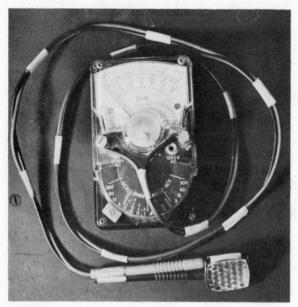

Light Meter

12. Raise the cardboard all the way allowing the beam to illuminate the film and object.

NOTE: Exposure time is by experiment based on Laser output, reflective characteristics and size of object, brightness of beams, age of film and chemicals, and temperature of D-19. With a 5mW Laser, a reading for the object beam and a reading 2x to 5x brighter than this for the reference beam, fresh film and chemicals, D-19 at 68° and a light colored object we have used a 20 second exposure.

We do not recommend turning your laser on and off with each exposure. Use your cardboard shutter to begin and end your exposure. This will help to insure that your laser is operating at its highest output.

You can mentally count the seconds: One thousand . . . Two thousand . . . Three . . . thousand.

13. Lower the cardboard shutter, remove the film and place in the D-19 developer emulsion side up and agitate checking every 30 seconds to see if the exposed part of the film is a light to medium gray. This check can be made by holding the film over the safelight and observing the contrast between the exposed part and the clear edge that was hidden from the light by the Film Holder. If the film does not turn gray within 5 minutes development time,

your exposure was much too short (or you may have left the cardboard block in the reference beam), and conversely if your film goes too dark within the first minute of development, your exposure was too long. Optimum time in the developer is between 2 to 3 minutes.

14. When the film is dark enough, place it in the stop bath of water and agitate for 30 seconds.

15. Remove from stop bath and agitate the film in the fixer for two minutes.

    If you plan to bleach your hologram you would not fix (see pages 66-68) for two different techniques.

16. You can quickly check to see if there is any image at all by holding the film over a small light bulb and tilting the film around while looking through it. If everything was correct, you should see a rainbow of colors. If you do not see this rainbow, it is a sure bet that there is no image and skip to step #18.

17. Wash film for 10 minutes under cold water faucet, agitate in Photo-Flo solution for 30 seconds, and let dry making sure the emulsion is not in contact with any surface.

18. No image or poor image can be caused either by vibrations during exposure, insecure object, or poor contrast of beam ratios.

Basic Photographic Supplies

TO RECONSTRUCT

Put the film back in the Film Holder with the emulsion toward the object. Remove the object. Replace the Beam Splitter with the Object Direction Mirror. This will put all the Laser light into the reference beam. Adjust the components so that the reference beam through the lens illuminates the film. Look through the film and see the image of the object in its original location on the table. You may have to slightly rotate the Film Holder in relation to the reference beam because of emulsion shrinkage.

You can achieve very good reconstruction using a point light source, such as a slide projector or a high intensity lamp with a 5770Å narrow band pass filter appendix taped behind a piece of cardboard with a ¼" hole punched in it. This assembly taped over the light source will result in a semi-coherent playback source.

You might want to try the following experiment. After you have made a good hologram do **not** remove the object from its position on the isolation table. Place the hologram back in the film holder with reference beam incident on the hologram. The reconstructed image of the object is seen superimposed on the object. If the reference beam is blocked the original object is seen through the hologram. Now proceed to block the reference and object beams alternately. You will find that in a completely darkened room it is difficult to distinguish between the real object and the reconstructed holographic image. Now adjust the hologram in the holder until the two are perfectly superimposed. Try pressing gently on the object with your fingertip. Notice the fringes at the point of contact. You have just performed stored beam holographic interferometry. A subject beyond the scope of this booklet but a very important process used widely today in the testing of mechanical components.

BASIC REFLECTION HOLOGRAM

TO SET UP: (Refer to illustration)

1. Roughly position **Laser, Direction** Mirror, and Film Holder (with the nylon screws on the opposite side of the object area).

2. Measure overall distance from Laser to Film as 32″ making sure of the 30° angle of reflection off the mirror. This will make reconstruction easier, for the reconstruction beam will not be in the way of the person viewing the hologram. You can try smaller angles but 30° to 45° is the extreme because of the tolerance of the emulsion.

3. Put a piece of white cardboard in the Film Holder and position the lens to fill the cardboard using the technique described in the Transmission set up.

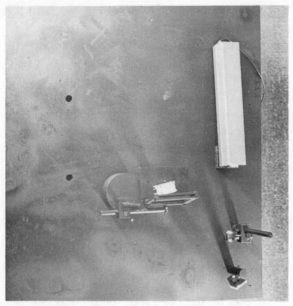

Single Beam Reflection Set-up

4. Place your object (a solid white object no larger than 3″ deep, 3″ tall and 4″ wide) as close to the Film Holder as possible and within the film frame.

5. Take out the white cardboard and see that the object is within the film frame, rotate the object until you like the position and secure it with a drop of epoxy or non-hardening modeling clay.

6. Put a piece of black cardboard in front of the Laser as a shutter. In the dark with only the green safe light on, place the film in the holder with the emulsion facing the object. Step back for a minute to let the table stop moving.

NOTE: No beam ratios to figure — there is only one beam. The light passing through the plate or film towards the object is the reference beam. The light scattered back towards the emulsion by the object is the **object beam**. The two counter flowing waves interfere with one another to produce the stationary interference pattern recorded by the hologram. Using the set up shown on page 61 be sure to keep your object as close to the film plane as possible, but be careful not to scratch the emulsion when you are inserting or removing the film.

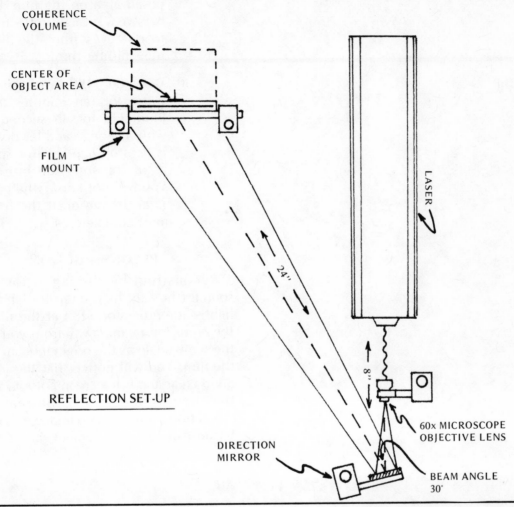

COHERENCE
VOLUME

CENTER OF
OBJECT AREA

FILM
MOUNT

LASER

24"

8"

60x MICROSCOPE
OBJECTIVE LENS

REFLECTION SET-UP

DIRECTION
MIRROR

BEAM ANGLE
30°

7. Lift the black cardboard, suspend it in the beam for a mental count of 10, lift the cardboard all the way out exposing the film, count mentally the exposure seconds, and replace the cardboard shutter to stop exposure. Exposure is short, between 5 and 10 seconds.

8. Develop for about 5 minutes in D-19 checking with the safelight for a **very** dark, almost black ex-

posed area on the film. Remember, we want light reflecting back to our eyes from the film, not transmitting through it.

10. **DO NOT FIX**!! Wash in running water for ten minutes, rinse in Photo-Flo for 30 seconds, wipe with a sponge and let dry. There is no stop gap test for spectrum as in transmission holograms. You will not know whether there is an image until the film is almost completely dry.

RECONSTRUCTION

Reconstruct by shining a point light source (the sun, high intensity lamp, flash light; slide projector, etc.) at the film with the emulsion facing away from you and at the same angle as the original beam that lit the film. You will notice that the image is quite clear and has a green color to it. Turn the film around to see the real image projection. (If there is no image, it is usually because of object movement .)

9. EXPERIMENTS

In all these illustrations, no attempt at scale has been made, and a certain amount of component fabrication is necessary on some of the set-ups.

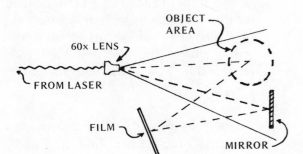

DIVISION OF AMPLITUDE TRANSMISSION HOLOGRAM

This type of hologram uses only one lens and a large mirror. Part of spread beam hits the object and goes to the film forming the object beam, and part of the beam hits a mirror which directs that portion to the film forming the reference beam.

These holograms yield greater resolution. But, with this resolution you get less depth of field or Coherence Volume. Also, the reference beam/object beam angle is very small making this almost an in-line hologram which puts the reconstruction beam almost in your eyes.

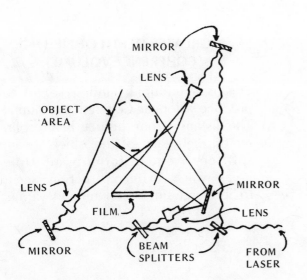

MULTIPLE OBJECT BEAM TRANSMISSION HOLOGRAM

By splitting the object beam, you can light the object from many different angles achieving lighting effects more akin to conventional photographic lighting techniques. But remember that the distance from the first beam splitter through each of the other beam splitters to the film must be equal.

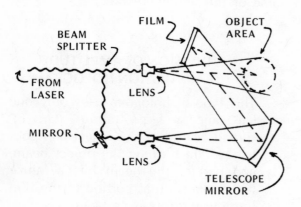

REAL IMAGE PROJECTION TRANSMISSION HOLOGRAM

Any hologram has the real image waves emerging from it. These waves are usually very distorted. Here is a set up that can produce a good real image.

The telescope mirror collimates the beam so that instead of a cone of light for the reference beam, you have a tube of light. After setting up to view the virtual image, the film is rotated 180° horizontally to view the real image.

NOTE:

Actually by using the dish mirror (approx. 50" f.l.) you create a slightly converging reference beam. You can playback with filtered light source as usual. The dish mirror can also be used to make real image reflection type holograms.

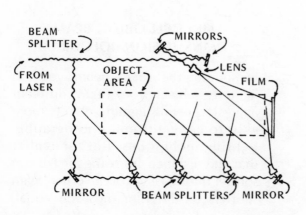

GREATER DEPTH OF FIELD (COHERENCE VOLUME)

This is a multiple lighting set-up to produce a longer Coherence Volume. The distance from the first beam splitter through each of the object beam splitters is equal, forming multiple areas which, in reconstruction, seem to be a large single Coherence Volume.

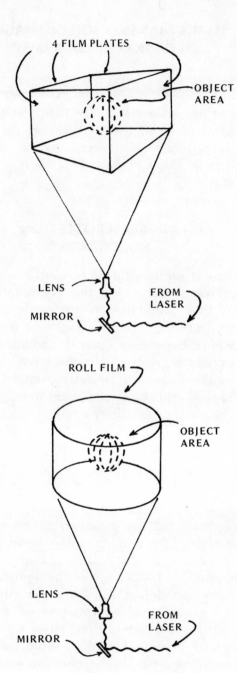

360° TRANSMISSION HOLOGRAMS

There are two ways to achieve 360° views of an object, and both use either the simpler Division of Amplitude (pg 63) technique in which your object and reference beam would both come down from the top; or split beam technique to independently light the object and produce a reference beam.

The first illustration uses four 4 x 5" pieces of film and the second uses 5" wide roll film that has the same emulsion as the plates and can be obtained from AGFA and Kodak.

The object area is smaller with the four plates but stabilizing of the roll film is difficult (try using a plexiglas tube, tape the film, emulsion facing in, on the outside and let it stabilize for 5 min. or more before exposure).

NOTE:

In the Division of Amplitude technique for 360° the light which reflects from the object to the film is the object beam. The light which misses the object and goes directly to the film is, by definition, the reference beam.

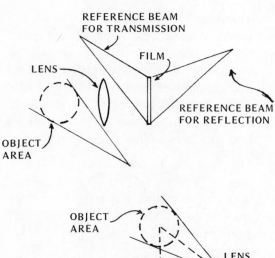

REFERENCE BEAM
FOR TRANSMISSION

FILM

LENS

REFERENCE BEAM
FOR REFLECTION

OBJECT
AREA

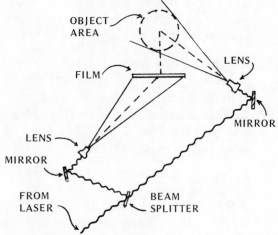

OBJECT
AREA

LENS

FILM

MIRROR

LENS

MIRROR

FROM
LASER

BEAM
SPLITTER

IMAGE TRANSMISSION OR IMAGE REFLECTION HOLOGRAMS

By placing a large lens between the object and the film with the center of the object and the film plane at the focal point of the lens, an image is formed that when reconstructed, lies half in and half out of the hologram plate.

TWIN-BEAM REFLECTION HOLOGRAMS

This is pretty straight forward but remember to balance the beam ratios as in a transmission hologram and measure the distances. Exposure times will be dependent upon the brightness of the beams after the ratios have been established. Here object movement is critical. This is a good setup to try the real image (see page 64).

10. BLEACHING

Holograms that are bleached are termed **Phase** Holograms and are often considerably brighter than conventional amplitude holograms. The following bleaching process has been developed by AGFA for their Scientia emulsion 8E75. This reversal process utilizes the desensitized silver halide residue for making the phase holograms. This method produces bright, low-noise holograms, which also do not easily fade. The image contrast is almost as high as that of conventional amplitude holograms. No special developers are required.

STANDARD BLEACH
PROCEDURE

1. Develop for 5 min. with average darkening.
2. Agitate in stop bath for 2 min. (I percent solution of acetic acid).
3. Wash for 5 minutes (check over light for spectrum)
4. Bleach for 2 minutes in:

   5 g of potassium bichromate
   5 ml of concentrated sulphuric acid in 1 litre of distilled water

5. Wash for 5 minutes

6. Clear for 1 minute in:

   50 g of sodium sulphite (anhyd.)
   1 g of sodium hydroxide in 1 litre of distilled water

7. Wash for 5 minutes
8. Desensitize in:

   880 g ethyl alcohol
   100 g distilled water
    20 g glycerine
   120 mg of potassium bromide
   200 mg phenosafrinine

9. Rinse briefly in ethyl alcohol and let dry

AN IMPORTANT NOTE

You might want to try another new method of bleaching. Carefully prepare some bromine water by following this simple but dangerous formula:

Dilute approximately two ounces of liquid bromine in one quart of water. Be very, very careful for bromine can easily burn the skin and the vapors are extremely toxic. The bromine will require up to 72 hours to be dispersed sufficiently to produce a solution of approximately 6%. Extreme caution should be maintained while handling the liquid.

After you have developed and fixed your hologram immerse it in a standard Photo-Flo solution (Photo-Flo is available at any camera store) for about one minute. Then, while the hologram is still wet, place it into the bromine water and observe the plate or film become transparent. (Depending on the strength of the solution more or less time will be required.) Then return to Photo-Flo and dry as usual. We strongly suggest that you use bromine outdoors, because the vapor tends to linger in a closed area, causing a very unpleasant odor.

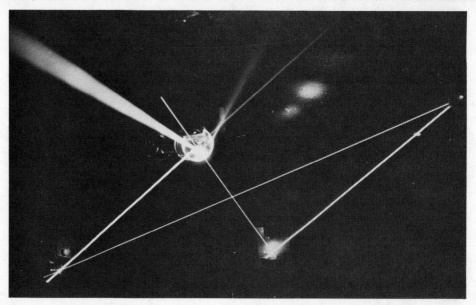

Laser Light Reflecting From Three Mirrors Towards Central Beam Splitter.

NOTE

All photographic films come from the manufacturer with development inhibiting coating, not unlike the preservatives which are added to food to prevent or retard spoilage. This coating keeps the film from spoiling while it is stored. If you wish you can remove this coating and thus hypersensitize the plate or film for a few hours by the simple procedure described here. This procedure temporarily increases the effective speed or light sensitivity of the film about three or four times without a gain in "noise". In practical terms this will make it possible to increase the size of your film so as to make holograms up to 8″ x 10″ with a low power laser. The procedure is as follows: Before exposing your film immerse it for approximately 2 minutes in a solution of water containing 3 drops of 28% ammonia per liter of water containing a wetting agent such as Photo-Flo. The solution should be kept at room temperature. After the film is completely wet, remove it from the solution and let it dry without sponging. **Remember, that the film must be handled in complete darkness.** The film must be exposed before more than a few hours have elapsed. Proceed to expose your treated film, keeping in mind that the exposure time can be decreased for a small hologram or conversely that you can make a larger one in the same amount of time it usually takes to make a smaller one. If you wish to increase your speed even further — approximately 10 times — you can develop your film in Dektol which has been heated to 100 C. This latter procedure will add considerable "noise" but it is worth experimenting with for unusual situations.

11. APPENDIX

GLOSSARY

Absorption Hologram — A hologram which **diffracts** light by means of small patterns of exposed emulsion in the form of silver residue.

Angstrom Unit — One ten billionth of a meter; one tenth of a nanometer. abbrev. Å.

Argon Ion Laser — A continuous wave gas laser which is capable of emitting light in various wavelengths of both blue and green light, usually more powerful and more expensive than a helium-neon type laser.

Coherence Volume — That volume of space in which an object may be placed and be expected to make a successful hologram; is defined by the tolerable path difference of the reference and object beams; also referred to as coherence length or depth.

Coherent — Implies a definite phase relationship between waves of light or other radiation being emitted.

Constructive Interference — The effects resulting from a superimposition of coherent wavelengths of light, for example, where a crest is superimposed on a crest.

Continuous Wave — CW. In referring to lasers this means that the energy emitted is continuous; a CW laser can be turned on and off like a normal light bulb unlike a ruby laser which emits its energy in pulses sometimes lasting less than a fraction of a billionth of a second.

Destructive Interference — The effects of the superimposition of a crest over a trough. The higher amplitude of the crest is cancelled by the lower amplitude of the trough. This occurs frequently when the waves of light are out of phase.

Electron — A stable elementary particle having a negative charge. The electron orbits about the nucleus of the atom at a given distance from the nucleus. If an electron is raised to a higher energy level, i.e. more distant from the nucleus, by an energy input, then the electron will give off energy as it falls back to a lower energy level. This energy is sometimes visible light.

Electromagnetic Radiation — EMR — Can be defined as waves of emitted energy characterized by the coexistence of electric and magnetic fields being propagated through air at approximately 186,000 miles per second. The visible light region is a very, very miniscule portion of the entire EM spectrum.

Etalon — An optical component made of fused quartz; sometimes used on a laser to filter out all other modes and insure pure monochromaticity and thus greatly increasing the coherence volume.

Excited State — The condition of an electron when it has been raised to a higher energy level by some ·external force. In a laser the force is electrical energy from the power supply.

Fringe (**s**) — A pattern of light and dark bands caused by the constructive and destructive interference of waves of light which is recorded in the holographic film emulsion.

Dennis Gabor — A Hungarian-born psysicist, the discoverer of the holographic technique and father of holography; proved that the phase information of light reflected or transmitted by an object could be captured by the interference of monochromatic, coherent light.

Ground State — The state of lowest energy of an atomic or molecular system.

Helium-Neon Laser — A continuous wave gas laser emitting light in the visible red region at 6328 Å; also the least expensive and most common laser.

Hertz — A unit of frequency in the International System of Units. It is equal to one cycle per second, 1 CPS.

Hologram — A photograph which contains information about intensity and phase of light reflected by an object. When illuminated at the correct angle with a sufficiently coherent source it will yield a diffracted wave which is identical in amplitude and phase distribution with the light reflected from the original object. The resultant three dimensional image can be viewed or photographed.

Holography — The technique of capturing, on photo-sensitive material, the image of an object which contains the amplitude, wavelength and phase of the light reflected by that object. The result is a three dimensional image of that object.

In-Line Hologram — A type of hologram in which the reference beam is brought to the holographic film at the same angle or on axis with the object beam; a single beam arrangement.

Image Hologram — A type of hologram which utilizes a lens to focus the object information onto the film plane. A hologram is made of the object as imaged by the lens.

Krypton-Argon Ion Laser — A continuous wave gas laser which can lase in the blue, green and red region; is more powerful and more expensive than the heliumneon laser.

Laser — An acronym for light amplification by stimulated emission of radiation. It provides a source of light which can be phase coherent and an intense beam can be attained by use of resonance techniques.

Mode — One of several possible states of oscillation which may be sustained in a resonant system.

Multiplex Hologram — A type of hologram which is formed by integrating a large number of photographs in a holographic manner; integral photography; usually only provides horizontal parallax.

Nanometer — One billionth of one meter, 1×10^{-9} meter.

Noise — Any undesirable disturbance or spurious signal.

Off-Axis Reference Beam — A reference beam which travels a different path from the object or scene beam and which is brought to the holographic film from a different angle than the object or scene modulated beam; requires a twin beam arrangement.

Orthoscopic Image — That reconstructed image which **maintains** the same spatial relationships of the object(s) as they were when holographed; usually the virtual image.

Oscillation — A periodical change in the amount of energy contained in an electrical, atomic or mechanical system.

Phase — That portion of a period or cycle through which a quantity (in this case a wave of electromagnetic radiation) has proceeded from an arbitrary point, for example the crest or highest point in amplitude of its wavelength, to the next crest after passing through zero.

Phase Hologram — A hologram which **refracts** light by means of different thicknesses of a transparent substance; commonly, a bleached hologram.

Photon — A quantum or discrete package of Electromagnetic Radiation.

Plane Wave — A wave of coherent laser light before it is changed or scattered by interfering with an object. A reference beam is essentially a plane wave.

Population Inversion — The condition which occurs when the greater majority of electrons are in the higher energy level rather than the ground state.

Pseudoscopic Image — That reconstructed image which **reverses** the spatial relationships of the object(s) from that which it was when holographed; usually the real image.

Pulse Ruby Laser — A solid state laser the heart of which is a ruby rod comprised of aluminum oxide mixed with a small amount of chromium. When properly excited and amplified the ruby emits light in the visible red region. The ruby laser is a solid state laser. When pulsed it can emit powerful bursts of light energy commonly around 20 billionths of a second or 20 nanoseconds, thus, virtually eliminating the concern with object movement in holography.

Real Image — That image which is projected out from the hologram towards the viewer.

Reference Beam — That part of the laser beam which is not affected or changed by the object being holographed.

Reflection Hologram — A type of hologram which is constructed by causing the object beam and reference beam to interfere from opposite sides of the holographic film or plate. In order to view the reconstructed image incoherent light is **reflected** back towards the viewer from the hologram.

Resonant Cavity — A chamber or enclosure whose design and physical characteristics permit only energy of a specific frequency to be propagated.

Scene or Object Beam — That part of the laser beam which is sent to the object being holographed and which is subsequently changed or modulated by the object before interfering with the reference beam on the photosensitive material.

Spatial Coherence — That condition in which the light waves traveling through space are not only of the same frequency, but they are in phase in space.

TEM $_\infty$ — The lowest mode of oscillation in the laser; preferable because it gives most uniform illumination and is most stable mode of oscillation.

Temporal Coherence — That condition in which the light waves are monochromatic, i.e. each cycle of the wave takes exactly the same time to pass a given point in space.

Transmission Hologram — A type of hologram which is constructed by causing the object beam and reference beam to interfere from the same side of the holographic film or plate. In order to view the reconstructed image, semi-coherent filtered light or very coherent laser light is **transmitted** to the viewer through the hologram.

Transverse Wave — A wave motion in which the substance of the medium is displaced in a direction at right angles to the direction of propagation of the wave.

Virtual Image — That image which appears in the space behind the hologram.

Volume Hologram — A type of hologram in which the angle difference between the object beam and reference beam is equal to or greater than 90°. All reflection holograms are volume holograms.

Wavelength — The length or distance in the direction of travel of a wave motion between two arbitrary points in neighboring cycles having the same amplitude and phase.

EQUIPMENT CHECK LIST

1. Isolation Table

2. Darkroom

3. Optical Mounts
   - 3 Mirror Mounts
   - 2 Lens Mounts
   - Film Holder
   - Beam Splitter Mount

4. Light Meter

5. Photographic Supplies
   - Film
   - D-19 Developer
   - Fixer
   - Trays
   - Chemical Containers
   - Graduate
   - Funnel
   - Green Safelight
   - Photo Sponge
   - Timer
   - Tape Measure
   - Penlight

SCHOOLS

School of Holography
      San Francisco — Tel. (415) 285-9035
   * Director — Lloyd Cross

Lake Forest Holography Workshop
      Lake Forest College
      Illinois
      Director: Dr. Jeong

University of California at Los Angeles,
Extension Holography Classes
      Directors: Chris Outwater and
      Eric Van Hamersveld
      Tel. (213) 271-1186

* At this time Lloyd is not teaching Holography,
   but has begun the Multiplex Co. in San Francisco.

MANUFACTURERS AND DISTRIBUTORS OF HOLOGRAPHIC EQUIPMENT AND SUPPLIES

The companies listed below are dependable suppliers known to the authors of this guide. No attempt has been made to provide an exhaustive list of companies in this field.

- Edmund Scientific Co., 150 Edscorp Building, Barrington, N.J., 08007

  Edmund Scientific publishes an extensive catalog of supplies and equipment for the experimenter. We have used their optics and recommend them for their low cost, and quality. They also distribute inexpensive quality lasers and power supplies. Good people.

- Spectra Physics, 1250 West Middlefield Road, Mountain View, Calif., 94040

  We believe that Spectra Physics manufactures a high quality laser at a reasonable price. They are nice people who can be relied upon for information and advice.

- Holex Corporation, 2544 West Main Street, Norristown, Penn., 19401

  Holex produces and distributes high quality holograms and viewers at reasonable prices. They are also a good source of information and advice.

- Newport Research Corporation, 18235 Mt. Baldy Circle, Fountain Valley, California, 92708

  If you plan to buy all or some of your optics already assembled or isolation apparatus we recommend that you contact these people.

- Korad Division of Hadron, Inc., 2520 Colorado Ave., Santa Monica, Calif., 90404

  These people are a builder of high quality pulsed ruby lasers and complete holographic cameras. If you have a lot of money to spend by all means contact them. Great instruments if you have a use for them.

BIBLIOGRAPHY

H.J. Caufield, and Sun Lu, **The Applications of Holography.** Wiley (Interscience), New York, 1970.

H.P. Chambers and J.S. Courtney-Pratt, "Bibliography on Holograms," **J.Soc. Motion Pict. Telev. Eng.** 75, 373, 759 (1966).

J. B. DeVelis and G. O. Reynolds, **Theory and Applications of Holography.** Addison-Wesley, Reading, Massachusetts, 1967.

D. Gabor, "A New Microscopic Principle," **Nature**. 161, 77 (1948); "Microscopy by Reconstructed Wavefronts," **Proc. Roy. Soc.** A197, 454 (1949); "Microscopy by Reconstructed Wavefronts: II," **Proc. Phys. Soc.**, B64, 449 (1951).

W. E. Kock, **Lasers and Holography: An Introduction to Coherent Optics.** Doubleday, New York, 1969.

H. M. Smith, **Principles of Holography**. Wiley (Interscience), New York, 1969.

R. J. Collier, C. B. Burckhardt and L. H. Lin, **Optical Holography**. Academic Press, New York, 1971.

E. N. Leith and J. Upatnieks, "Reconstructed Wavefronts and Communication Theory," **J. Opt. Soc. Amer**. 52, 1123 (1962); "Wavefront Reconstruction with Continuous-Tone Objects," **J. Opt. Soc. Amer**. 53, 1377 (1963); Wavefront Reconstruction with Diffused Illumination and Three-Dimensional Objects," **J. Opt. Soc. Amer**. 54, 1295 (1964).

M. Born and E. Wolf, **Principles of Optics**, 3rd ed. Pergamon Press, Oxford, 1964.

F. B. Rotz and A. A. Friesem, "Holograms with Nonpseudoscopic Real Images," **Appl. Phys. Lett**. 8, 146 (1966).

G. W. Stroke, "White-Light Reconstruction of Holographic Images Using Transmission Holograms Recorded With Conventionally Focused Images and In-Line Background," **phys. Lett**. 23, 325 (1966).

E. N. Leith and J. Upatnieks, "Photography By Laser," **Scientific Am.** June, 1965.

K.S. Pennington, "Advances in Holography," **Scientific Am**. Feb 1968.